Exponential Theory

EXPONENTIAL THEORY

The Power of Thinking BIG

Aaron D. Bare

with N. Forbes Shannon

NEW YORK

LONDON • NASHVILLE • MELBOURNE • VANCOUVER

EXPONENTIAL THEORY

The Power of Thinking BIG

Published in New York, New York, by Morgan James Publishing. Morgan James is a trademark of Morgan James, LLC. www.MorganJamesPublishing.com

Aaron Bare/Aaron Bare, LLC
www.aaronbare.com

Proudly distributed by Ingram Publisher Services.

Morgan James BOGO™

A **FREE** ebook edition is available for you or a friend with the purchase of this print book.

CLEARLY SIGN YOUR NAME ABOVE

Instructions to claim your free ebook edition:
1. Visit MorganJamesBOGO.com
2. Sign your name CLEARLY in the space above
3. Complete the form and submit a photo of this entire page
4. You or your friend can download the ebook to your preferred device

ISBN 9781631956676 paperback
ISBN 9781631956683 ebook
Library of Congress Control Number:
2021940023

Cover Concept by:
Jonathan Limancoa

Cover and Interior Design by:
Chris Treccani
www.3dogcreative.net

Morgan James PUBLISHING **Builds** with... **Habitat for Humanity** Peninsula and Greater Williamsburg

Morgan James is a proud partner of Habitat for Humanity Peninsula and Greater Williamsburg. Partners in building since 2006.

Get involved today! Visit MorganJamesPublishing.com/giving-back

Dedicated to all those in pursuit of purpose; by asking questions, challenging assumptions and changing the world around you.
Carpe Diem!
—AB & FS

Dedicated to my family, who have supported my global innovation journey for the last 15+ years, to my children Bali and Maverick who inspire me to be part of the solution for our future, and to my parents, who instilled great values in me.
—AB

Dedicated to my Mom, who taught me to love telling stories.
—FS

Contents

Acknowledgments

Special thanks to Forbes Shannon for helping me draw out the stories for this book. Thanks to Alan "AP" Powell for keeping life interesting. Thanks to the mother of my children Jennifer Bare for always being there for me. Thanks to Russ Wall for the support. Thanks to Hannah Brodie and Jaya Chatterjee for the editing.

I also want to express extreme gratitude and appreciation for the support, mentorship, thought leadership, and/or conversations on innovation with: Aaron Richardson, Aaron Rodriquez, Abdu Daindridge, Adam Bremen, Adam Such, Adam Vigil, Alan "AP" Powell, Alan G. Rodbell, Alec Ross, Alex Osterwalder, Amir Glogau, Amy Rae, Andrew Cohn, Andrew Lampe, Andreas Bauer, Andrew Lombard, Dr. Angel Cabrera, Anna Sokolova, Antonio Dominquez, Anthony Bajores, Art Hamilton, Aish Narang, Ash Maurya, Austin Jack, Bali Bare, Beau Lane, Bill Bare, Bill Lavidge, Dr. Bob Hisrich, Bob Stockwell, Bonnie Love, Boris Kodjoe, Brad Tilford, Brent Sebold, Brian Burt, Brian Mohr, Bryan Sperber, Candi Luciano, Carl Yamoshiro, Cheri Reeves, Cheryl Heller, Chris Farrell, Chris Jester, Chris Johnson, Chris Rawlinson, Chris Voss, Chris Yoo, Christina Ngo, Christopher Deutch, Clare Boyd, Craig Nealy, Darren Wilson, Dan Zlaket, Daniel Epstein, Dave McLurg, David Johnson, David Barnett, Daymond John, Dr. Denis LeClerc, Dennis Prince, DeVonte Rosero, Donald Hannah, Douglas Griffen, Drew Trojanowski, Donavon Ostrom, Don Tapscott, Elle Shelley, Eric Hawkins, Eric Ries, Eric Trappen, Erron Boes, Frankie Jaramilla, Frank Busch, Fedrik Carlstrom, Francine Hardaway, Francisco Palao Reinés, George Grombacher,

Gerd Leonhard, Gerhard Meier, Glenn Hammer, Gonzalo De La Melena, Admiral Hal Pittman, Hala Al Kasm, Hannah Brodie, Heath McCarter, Heidi Lee, Humberto Espinosa, Jaclyn Kleiner, Jared Cohen, Jaraslav Dokoupil, Jeffrey Guldner, Jeffrey Gittomer, Jeffrey Pruitt, Dr. Jeff Walls, Jen Kaplan, Jennifer Bare, Ji Mi Choi, Jim Collins, John Fees, John Hagel, Jim Lane, Jim Prendergast, Jimmy Hutchinson, Jimmy Walker, John Santry, John Smart, Jon Gowar, Jon Tull, Jonathan Bonghi, Jonathan Hegrenes, Jonathan Keyser, Jonathan Limancoa, Jonathan Lines, Jonscott Turco, Joshua Husk, Justin Bachman, Justin Choi, Dr. Karen Walsh, Kate Robertson, Katie Clemens, Katie Perrine, Keld Jensen, Ken Mulligan, Ken Kendrick, Kenja Hassan, Kent Langley, Kerry Dunne, Kerwin Brown, Kirill Eremenko, Lieb Bolel, Linda Capcara, Liz Pellet, Malcolm Gladwell, Marc Goodman, Marsha Bare, Dr. Mary Sully de Luque, Matt O'Brien, Matthew Shuman, Maverick Bare, Max Hansen, Mel Hawkins, Michael Blazina, Michael Davidson, Michael Gerber, Michael Southworth, Dr. Neta Kela Madar, Dr. Netra Chhetri, Nicole Spracale, Noah Barrasso, PJ Bouchard, Paige Maurer Wheeler, Patrick McDermott, Pascal Finette, Patti Dubois, Paul Saffo, Peter Diamandis, Peter Theil, Randy Kendrick, Ray Kurzweil, Reed Glick, Dr. Robert Stralser, Dr. Robert Cialdini, Ron Williams, Rich Hempel, Rich Nickel, Richie Norton, Rick Stilgenbauer, Ryan Allis, Ryan Garmers, Safi Bahcall, Salim Ismael, Samuel Mueller, Sandra Watson, Dr. Sanjeev Khagram, Sara Ragland, Scott Foreman, Scott McIntosh, Shamshad Khan, Shawn Seaton, Sidnee Peck, Simon Kavanagh, Simon Sinek, Seth Godin, Smoke Wallin, Dr. Sogol Homayoun, General Spider Marks, Dr. Stefan Michel, Steve Blank, Steve Chucri, Steve Giusto, Steve Loy, Steve Moak, Steven Olson, Sunil Narang, Susan Halverson, T. Ryan Fitzgerald, Tasha Boyd-Jones, Thomas Shumann, Tim Leake, Timothy Ferriss, Trip Hawkins,

Toby Farmer, Todd Woods, Tom Collins, Tom Fulcher, Tony Feiter, Uwe Steinwender, Velma Treyham, Vielka Atherton, Will Overstreet, Wellington Reiter, and Zach Ferres.—AB

Read More, Lead More

> *"Not all readers are leaders, but all leaders are readers."*
> **—Harry Truman**

A guide to reading and understanding any book, including this book:

1. Take notes in the margins
2. Reflect on how you can apply each story on your own life
3. Highlight points of interest, put stars next to important points and come back to them
4. Use the book as a journal
5. Answer the questions posed by the author
6. Dig deep, read books in the bibliography to further understand the subject matter
7. Find a place to read and continue to read in that spot
8. Brief the book first, read the titles and get the gist before diving deep
9. Shut the outside world out
10. Give the book to someone else, pay it forward
11. Create a group to read the book together
12. Share quotes and messages to connect with other like-minded people online

A Note from N. Forbes Shannon

> *"The test of a first-rate intelligence is the ability to hold two opposing ideas in mind at the same time and still retain the ability to function. One should, for example, be able to see that things are hopeless yet be determined to make them otherwise."*
> **– F. Scott Fitzgerald**

As a young man, I was very successful on any standard. I was a Coca-Cola Scholar, the Valedictorian of my high school class, my high school's Martin Luther King Jr. award winner for service and leadership, and the National Civic League's 2011 All America Teen of the Year. I had my choice of universities (Michigan, Chicago, or Toronto) and I was certainly on my way to do something great to change the World.

Instead, I took an unconventional path and went to Barrett Honors College at Arizona State University (ASU), moving all the way across the country to find my life's purpose. I created a new identity at ASU as a writing fellow and an entrepreneurship and innovation fellow. I even started going by my middle name Forbes. I created a weekly comedy show (which became the largest performing group on campus), and I developed a duality to my life that most college kids do, balancing schoolwork with "extra-curricular activities." Life was great.

As I got older and deeper into college, the divide between the two sides of my personality grew deeper, and I struggled with what

I now know was manic depression. I was oft bouncing between the outgoing and productive maniac and the disappearing introvert. After graduation, I was on a downward spiral, under employed and stuck in a cycle of personal trauma. My two best friends (also my roommates) had both died in the span of a single year—one to suicide and another to an opioid overdose. There was a storm cloud hanging over my head holding me powerless.

My mental health was, unsurprisingly, spiraling. Every day I lived in fight or flight, just trying to make it through another day to toss and turn from a night of highs and lows. I was exhausted. I lost all interest in my passions, hobbies, and friendships. In this period of my life, no matter how many people I surrounded myself with, I still felt very alone.

I was on and off psychiatric medications, mis-labelled and mis-diagnosed. Ex-girlfriends each had their own diagnoses for me, and one went so far to call me a narcissist. I sought out therapy to make sure I wasn't on the socio-pathic spectrum as I re-discovered my ability to empathize. Every time I felt like I was making progress, a few months later I would have a major setback. First there was the legal troubles from alcohol and drug use. Then there was that involuntary stint in the mental hospital. Between suicide watch and house arrest I realized I was so focused on just survival that I mortgaged all my goals and my purpose of making a difference in the world.

As I shaved in front of the mirror before work one morning, re-living my life story, I asked myself, "How did my life end up here?"

———

I figured if I was to re-write my life story, I should find some-body that has a life I admire and pick their brain. I wrote down a list of former mentors, professors, and bosses, and started making my way down the list—calling and asking each of them if they'd want to grab coffee. A couple made time for me, and one of them was Aaron.

I met Aaron a couple of years before at ASU. Aaron was facil-itating (and the creator of) Startup School, part of ASU's bid to become the #1 Most Innovative School in the country. On the first day of my entrepreneurship and innovation fellowship, Aaron gave out his cell phone number to the cohort and encouraged us to get in touch. He said, "If I can help you, please give me a call, but 99% of you won't take me up on this offer." If it was a test, I passed, because a week later we were regularly getting coffee together. I was the one percent that took him up on it. I found great motivation in his interest in me.

Step one of re-writing my story was creating a new routine, surrounding myself with new friends, and committing to actions to get back into the growth mindset that I had thrived in years earlier. As Aaron put it, I needed to get beyond just a growth mindset, yet find my own "exponential mindset."

Over time, Aaron helped me find clarity, purpose, and mean-ing in my regular struggles. I began to learn from these moments and adapt, change, upgrade my software, and challenge myself to overcome things that regularly held me back. Aaron cut through challenges with razor sharp logic and common sense, removing emotion and creating purpose with each conversation. We talked about everything: politics, climate change, inequities, global issues, relationships, comedy, health, music, and art. Aaron has this intangible sixth sense or something where it felt like the rest of the World was moving in slow motion to him. The juice, the

X-factor, whatever you want to call it—this guy has it. When we reconnected, my outlook on life started to improve and I began to think bigger about my own potential.

So, when life got tough, I continued to turn to Aaron and start to understand how he took complex subjects and simplified them while maintaining empathy for both sides. Like F. Scott Fitzgerald, I was on a quest for first rate intelligence.

Throughout our conversations, Aaron said he wanted to take his exponential mindset, beliefs, and attitudes he'd built up over the years and figure out how to get them to the masses. I had already learned so much, and my life was improving just by talking about these ideas, that I insisted we write a book. I was, after all, a writer's fellow in college and my intuition told me this project would be life changing for not only myself, but for those that got the chance to experience it too.

"Have you ever written a book before?" Aaron asked me.

"Uh…no, but I've written a lot of really funny sketches, can't be that different."

———

Our first attempt at writing the book was a rough one. Turns out, writing a book is a lot more difficult than writing sketches. One time, Aaron was seriously doubting himself and said, "who am I to think I can help millions of people?"

"Well, this has all helped me a ton. We can't give up on this book, this needs to be shared with the world."

We finished our first book, *Reimagining Innovation,* in 2020 during the first COVID-19 lockdown. We were both starting over like the rest of the world. Aaron had been on a global speaking tour that got cancelled and I was managing a restaurant that was forced to close. It was then we decided this was our chance. For the entirety of the stay-at-home order we worked incessantly on finishing that book. We turned what everyone saw as a negative and turned it into our own opportunity.

Reimagining Innovation was a book about complex problem solving but we realized what we were talking about wasn't just a way to solve problems. We had a breakthrough as a higher message appeared to explain life, leadership, progress, change, adaptation, success, and failure. We stumbled upon a new message, ***Exponential Theory: The Power of Thinking Big.***

Exponential Theory became broadly compelling because we managed to capture Aaron's optimistic outlook and his capability to break down complex ideas with global ramifications into simple executable ideas. We wrote about, and actively practice together, creating empathy for all sides of a problem. Of all the impressionable traits of Aaron's character, the one that most improved my own life was Aaron's motivation to help others succeed. As he puts it, "Don't split the pie when you can grow the pie," —a thread woven throughout the book that inclusivity is significantly more powerful than exclusivity. Diversity improves every idea, and there is always a better way.

At one point near the end of the writing process over a sushi dinner in Las Vegas I told him the Padawan (me) would eventually become stronger than the Jedi Master (him) and—I'll never forget this—he laughed said "Forbes, nothing would make me happier." I pressed him for a reason, and it was simple to him: "When you get better, I inherently get better too. When you help people, I help people. We need an army of people to take this challenge. If people read our book, and in turn do good in their lives or it nudges them in the right direction, then we're making a difference in the World."

———

Understanding and practicing the *Exponential Theory* changed my entire life trajectory from a flat line to accelerating growth. They say some people bounce hard when they hit rock bottom, and *Exponential Theory* showed me that I'm one of those people. Frankly, it showed me I could be whatever I want—my life is my own story to write.

The exponential mindset, beliefs, and attitudes behind *Exponential Theory* taught me to accept and love myself. When I was first diagnosed as bipolar, I resented it and how it made me feel. Somedays, or even months at a time, I felt out of control. I was embarrassed and ashamed. However, with *Exponential Theory* I learned to not view my mental illness as a disability, but rather a superpower.

Through *Exponential Theory* my ambition returned, and I turned my mania into running a marathon, completing a cross-country stand-up comedy tour, a feature length documentary, a self-written and produced music album, becoming a certified Oxford leadership coach, a community champion for the city of Phoenix, and of course, an author—all by the age of 25. Once I embraced my flaws, no one could use them against me. Once I embraced them as super-powers, no one could stand in my way.

My life has gotten exponentially better. What's beautiful about this book and the corresponding framework is that it can deliver to us what we need when we don't know what we need ourselves. *Exponential Theory*, in my opinion, became a self-help book where Aaron's ideas reach through the page interweaved with stories about some of the greatest innovators and entrepreneurs to live on our planet.

I chalk my mentality shift to what Aaron practices every day and presents in the book—gratitude and hope. This message gave me an identity and a belonging to a group of people that will change the world. A group that will stand up for what's right and make the world a better place. As we wrote in this book, the future belongs to a few people that are willing to challenge the status quo and make the necessary changes. I'm proud to say that because of *Exponential Theory* I am part of these changemakers, heroes, disruptors, innovators, entrepreneurs, and future CEO's dismantling what does not work for the whole to help the world heal from the trauma asserted by a few.

What waits for you, too, on the other end of this book will be truly life changing, even if you're starting at rock bottom or on the top of your own mountain, there is always a higher peak. You'll be well on your way to living a life of abundance by just reading the book alone. It's not always easy to be positive and up-beat, but I've found it's much easier to lead a life of gratitude and hope than it is to live a life without them.

To me *Exponential Theory* pulls no punches. It shoots straight and gives the reader everything they need to succeed, on a personal, professional, and organizational level. It's written with love, passion, and a bit of humor. It's as much art as it is informative. While this book will teach us each something different, it'll teach us all the same thing, best summed up by a famous Adidas slogan: impossible is nothing.

Welcome to the future.

Love,
Forbes

Chapter 0.

Welcome to the Future

"No problem can withstand the assault of sustained thinking."
—Voltaire

Welcome to the Future

> *"Innovation distinguishes between a leader and a follower."*
> **—Steve Jobs**

With the rise of digital technology, business moves at unprecedented speeds and now runs at an exponential pace. This pace is wreaking havoc on the business landscape as we know it. Disruption has brought "too big to fail" companies to their knees in a matter of months, and it has made some industries obsolete. Any company or leader that doesn't move at an exponential pace will be crushed by new, massively transformative exponential organizations.

These organizations are quickly expanding their purpose and invading new industries every day. Guides like Bill Gates, Jeff Bezos, Elon Musk, and others continue to provide us with road maps for how to navigate the exponential horizon. Through a collection of ten ways of thinking big, we have created a formula to navigate the disruption, think big, and make the necessary changes for your company to thrive and the world to survive.

Thinking big and exponential theory—combined with emerging technologies and accelerated change—will not only disrupt the world but also gives us a chance to save it. It is time for a new generation of leadership—for leaders who are purposeful, conscious, digital, and above all, exponential. A leader focused on the entire system. No longer can we ignore the signs of bad decisions or small thinking by leaders. *Exponential Theory* outlines how our decisions impact an integrated system and why we must start to consider all the stakeholders to survive which ultimately will drive more growth, abundance, and profit. Join us on a journey to reimagine the future of leadership through exploring exponential theory.

Disrupt Yourself or Be Disrupted

My journey to discover the exponential theory began when I was 20 years old. I dared to sneak into the University of Notre Dame's Career Center in hopes of landing an interview for a Chicago internship, even though I didn't even attend the university. However, while at Notre Dame I discovered a poster of Semester at Sea and fell in love with the idea of traveling around the world. That day, I didn't get the internship, but I started on a new adventure.

Less than a year later, I left home to circumnavigate the world, venture into the unknown, understand the world, reinvent my potential, and expand my own self-limiting box. I flew to the Bahamas and boarded the SS Universe, a 554-foot ocean liner built in 1953. As I departed, I knew I would not be in a familiar environment again until I had it made it all the way back around the world. At that point in life, I didn't know a single person who had traveled outside the United States, let alone any of my fellow travelers on this voyage. I stepped into a new world and began challenging myself in new ways every day.

This was my first step into exploring the uncomfortable, with no safety net. My greatest period of growth began by boarding the SS Universe that day. My growth came when I realized I was all alone, and I continued onward and chose growth over comfort. I was already a thousand miles from home, and still headed further away. I wonder if an astronaut headed toward the moon might feel the same way.

The excitement was subdued by the FEAR (False Evidence Appearing Real) I was experiencing. The expedition moved me in and out of 12 cultures on three continents over 120 days. Nearly half of those days were spent in the open waters in a giant social experiment, while the other half was spent exploring new countries, people, languages, and cultures. Every day opened my eyes to something new. New places, new situations, and new people, all forced me to continuously rewire my brain and grow. In doing this, I started to open up the limited beliefs from my modest midwestern upbringing. I was recreating my worldview and I was doing it quickly. My dreams got bigger! Suddenly, for the first time I believed that I could accomplish great things and make a difference by stepping up to challenges that presented themselves. My path had been forged and unfolded in front of me as opportunities magically presented themselves as my thoughts began to play out in the real world. I started developing my purpose. I started attracting the people and opportunities I needed into my life. The path becomes clear when your purpose is clear.

However, past anchors and conditioning prevented my box from expanding too quickly. For example, my high school English teacher had said to me, "Aaron, you are never going to amount to anything," and I believed her. My confidence had been shaken. I graduated in the bottom half of my high school class, with colleges only interested in my ability to play soccer. Soccer was my chance out of a career in construction, a likely profession for a midwestern high school graduate. Thankfully, I was recruited by many colleges for soccer, ultimately making the safe choice to stay home and attend the school that my high school soccer coach started coaching. I thought that was the best option for me at the time.

In college, my thirst for knowledge accelerated. I graduated with honors in three years. I continued to graduate school to earn a degree in Latin American Studies as I continued to see a bigger world. This would open the door to my ultimate education goal, getting my MBA from the Thunderbird School of Global Management. I achieved that 10 years later. Looking back, I now realize that intelligence has nothing to do with formal education or a classroom. Ironically, I found I learned more about life, and about how to excel in a life, in my time spent outside the classroom. As Elon Musk has said on many occasions, "Don't confuse schooling with education."

While these experiences served me well, I recognize that this is not everyone's experience. My experiences built the necessary confidence for me to open the door to many opportunities, including becoming the Entrepreneur-in-Residence at Thunderbird and eventually this experience opened the door to many other Universities and eventually led me to Singularity University at NASA Ames campus in Mountainview working with some of the most exponential entrepreneurs in the world. It also opened the door to facilitating innovation around the world with companies like WDHB, Hyper Island, and Kaos Pilot. Just as a shark will only grow to eight inches in a fish tank but will grow to more than eight feet in the ocean, I was soon swimming in a much bigger world.

I was obsessed with learning. I was curious how the world works, entrenched in a world of innovation with some of the best companies in the world. I also took nearly every course I could find, and rarely turned down any opportunity presented to me to explore new ways to think. I continued to expand my beliefs, purpose, and vision. I traveled, explored, and put myself into challenging situations. I wanted to see who I really was and what my potential could be. I grew my confidence to lead and leaned into difficult conversations. I continue to challenge myself to take on more.

For years, I looked for a sign from the outside world. However, it wasn't until I started to take a deeper journey within that I realized I already had the answers. Through a series of leadership development courses, I stopped looking to the outside world for validation. I learned to say "no." This helped me to avoid burnout and led me to take an introspective journey, which led me to Bali, Indonesia to spend time with some of the world's great energy healers. My energy needed recharging. I spent a day with a laughing Shaman, fasted for two weeks, and I spent time in a Buddhist monastery in silence. I also spent time in isolation in the wilderness. I realized my own self-love and self-worth were only set by myself. I became mindful and embraced the joy of missing out (JOMO). I shed excess ownership, weight, and simplified my whole life. I finally found freedom, living by my own terms.

I continued to travel, learn, grow, and educate myself, to learn how to talk to myself, to innovate myself, and to reimagine myself. As the world is a perfect picture of our own imagination, I became aware of my own intentions and my own fears holding me back from becoming everything I wanted to be. I was free to just be myself, and I accepted that I was good enough. I stepped into the present moment for the first time.

My new identity was set. I continued to create my future in a push and pull between my growing and limiting beliefs. A tug of war that with some positive self-talk, led me to personal, professional and organization growth. I became an adventurous paratrooper that dropped into companies to solve incredibly difficult problems with facilitation, design thinking, and systems thinking. I designed the perfect role for myself, and over time grew into thinking big and I stepped up to any challenge presented to me.

I began to embrace the powers of exponential theory, before I had a theory for it. I took responsibility for the creation of my outcomes. In my career, I've created a dozen companies, three non-profits, a half-dozen education programs, and three accelerators. I lost people money, made people money, and exited several startups. I continued to fail forward, learn, make mistakes, and grow.

On the journey, I become a global innovation facilitator working with companies like Daimler, Coca-Cola, and Google, learning and growing from some of the greatest corporate leaders in the world. I worked on projects that created billions in bottom line revenue. I travelled to all 50 states and over 90 countries. My limiting beliefs faded, and I found myself in the middle of wickedly complex problems and began to dismantle them and create solutions with relative ease. I began to impact the world in an exponential way. I found my purpose-to inspire those that I crossed paths with to think big and find their purpose. I began to surround myself with the right people, and I made sure they looked at the world the way I wanted to see it: as an optimistic, big thinker, which led to the writing this book.

> *"Watch your thoughts, they become your words; watch your words, they become your actions; watch your actions, they become your habits; watch your habits, they become your character; watch your character, it becomes your destiny."*
> **—Lao Tzu**

Much of our life is on autopilot by the way we feel about ourselves, our identity, and our belonging. We need to learn to better talk to ourselves. By the age of five, 90% of our neural pathways have been formed, leading to beliefs about how we deal with the world around us.[1] Understanding why our ancestry affects our decision-making process even today through subconscious bias will help us understand the power of thinking big and the need to become more conscious.

As I reflected while writing this book over the last 15 years, I began working on positive thoughts and stepping into an abundant and exponential future. I felt like I was discovering it and creating it at the same time. This book is a journey through stories I have collected on my life path woven into a process that will help others find their purpose by exploring their vision, values, beliefs, obstacles, and continuously iterating. As the idea of Exponential Theory emerged, I realized that I had conflict with the people in my life who didn't think big. I realized how thinking big did not leave time to worry about the small stuff. Conversely, I recognized that people who put time into understanding the big picture were much more conscious and made bigger impacts on the projects they worked on. With this simple epiphany, Exponential Theory was born. It was clear, I wanted to help others find their purpose and impact the world in a bigger way.

The book is chock-full of ideas that further explain Exponential Theory and can be applied to companies, industries, technology, people, relationships, negotiations, processes, and strategies. For the first time in my life, I am complete, whole, and happy to be exactly where I am. My clear vision is to share the power of thinking big with people who want to spend time on solving problems for the greater good. Beyond welcoming you to the future, I hope you take this journey to create a better world. My goal is to raise consciousness through thinking bigger, to create world peace, one mind at a time. I hope you can leave insignificant thoughts behind and focus on making a bigger impact. It all starts with a thought. It all starts right here.

Through my innovation journey to nearly every corner of Earth, I learned these seven universal truths. I hope you can reflect on them through the stories here within.

1. We are always right. To think is to create. Your perception is your reality.
2. We are our habits. How we spend our days is how we spend our lives. Focusing on personal habits and putting in the work will help us reach our goals.
3. Attitude is everything. It's not what happens to us, it's how we respond.
4. What we resist persists. Let it go! Forgive.
5. The goal is not the end. The journey is the reward. Enjoy the process.
6. Enjoy the moment. Now is all we've got. Be present.
7. We are all one. Love unconditionally.

Exponential Theory helped me understand the world, reinvent myself, my potential, and expand my own self-limiting box. This process was a great reset for me, and I hope this book creates a great reset for you. Hopefully, through this book, you can create a movement to become a leader in the future and become part of the much-needed solutions to solve the world's biggest challenges. Share this book and help create a world full of better leaders.

REFLECTION

The future is now. Today you start a journey to venture into the unknown, understand the world, reinvent your potential, and expand your own self-limiting box.

- What are your limiting beliefs you need to disrupt?
- What are the triggers to let you know you are outside your comfort zone?
- How do you spend your time? Take inventory.
- Write down everything on your mind. This will be important in the next chapter.

Chapter 1.

What is Exponential Theory?

"Imagination is the most powerful force in the universe."
—**Albert Einstein**

The Current Situation

Which should we cover first, the good news or the bad news?

The good news: the future is bright. The bad news: the present is not. Between human and civil rights issues, recovering from a pandemic, and a deteriorating planet, the clock looks like it is running out on us. Whether we recognize it or not, humans are at a critical point in their existence: adaptation or extinction.

With the polar ice caps melting, plastic filling our rising sea waters, level five hurricanes flooding our coastal cities[2], armies of violent tornadoes[3], and tsunamis crushing coastlines on a more regular basis[4], the natural world around us is in constant chaos. Global weirding continues to stress the world with extreme weather conditions, causing forest fires, droughts, heat spells (global warming), cold spells (global cooling), and pushing many species toward mass extinction.[5] We have seen a two-thirds decline in biodiversity in less than half a century due to environmental destruction.[6]

This has contributed to the emergence of zoonotic diseases such as Ebola and Covid-19.[7] Environmental destruction is exacerbated by the exponentially expanding population, as humans are moving into more congested urban spaces, yet at the same time now inhabit over three-fourths of the available land on Earth. Deserts are growing while farmland and forest are shrinking as our landscape continues to change from the environmental stress. Unsustainable farming practices are creating massive soil erosion and potentially the complete loss of usable soil in less than 60 years.[8] We've entered the Anthropocene, a new geologic time period, because of how drastically humans have altered our atmospheric, geologic, hydrologic, bio-spheric and other Earth systems.[9] Is extinction evident?

The world is also in a state of political unrest. Confidence in our political leaders is at an all-time low. Truth has become optional. The United States Capitol was taken over by insurgents for the first time since 1814.[10] Politics has been polarized by social media and news feeds anchor people into opposing opinions, further dividing society. Special interest groups influence both political parties and wreak havoc on democracy. Our interconnected networks have allowed hackers to expose the world's most secure information. The world is filled with wicked problems. Wicked problems are social or cultural problems that on the face appear nearly impossible to solve because, among other things, the overwhelming number of opinions or systems that are interwoven within them.[11]

The nuclear arms race is ongoing, as new powers like North Korea and Iran threaten the global power structure. The fight to end racial injustice and combat police brutality has gripped the United States and the world at large. Millennials have experienced two black swan economic crises as they come into the workforce, creating huge unemployment and underemployment for youth globally. We're in a defining moment of human existence, and we are as ill-prepared for it as we were for the economically devastating coronavirus pandemic. To some this will sound alarmist, but to others exponential theory will be a way to better explain the need for systemic change.

The universe is demanding and forcing change. However, humans are creatures resistant to change that anchor into bad routines and habits. For example, our body communicates to us, but we ignore it. When we eat the wrong things, our body tell us by giving us heartburn, gaining weight, and other skin and organ ailments. This is our body demanding dietary change. Medical Doctors can diagnose these ailments, but if the patient does not change their habits, cancer, heart attacks, and other more serious illnesses await. The world is crying out for change in much of the same way. However, things have gotten so dire we must ask ourselves, does the world have heartburn or are we having a heart attack?

Consider the people we know that struggle with abusive relationships, addiction, or criminal activity. As an outsider we can see the obvious need to change, but often those suffering are blinded by the norm of their habits or the group they identify and belong to. It's obvious when we criticize others behavior, yet we are not always so clear recognizing our own contribution to a system that is not working for all of us. Breaking this cycle, becoming more self-aware, and stepping outside of our comfort zones will be critical to dismantle the many systemic bad habits we fight. Nothing in the exponential theory happens inside our comfort zone and the universe continues to show the sickness. The good thing is, we have the cure, we just need to apply it.

With digitization—the process of using bits and bytes, or computers to replace the world around us—humans have unlocked exponential growth and our ability to create massive change. Technology is not the answer to all our problems, yet it provides a way to accelerate the response to every problem.

Exponential growth is the hockey stick growth that every company dreams about. Exponential is a rate of change that starts slow, but then skyrockets to infinity and beyond. Change used to be the only constant, but now even change itself is accelerating. Through thinking big, digitization, and accelerating change, the exponential theory proves that no problem will be too big to be solved—be it the climate, racial divides, social/political imbalances, economic crises, or access to healthcare—although they currently appear to be impossible or unfixable. As science teaches us, nothing is permanent, we are accelerating towards potential solutions to nearly every plaguing problem on this planet. The world is in a constant flux of change.

Leaders need to focus on their people, the planet, and purpose over profit. This is a call for conscious capitalism. Capitalism should not be in question, though exponential theory will articulate the need for it to be more conscious. There is no time but the present to employ exponential theory to create the needed change to survive and hopefully thrive with a new more compassionate and creative leader that leans into the current challenges.

Godspeed.

Exponential Theory

Exponential Theory states that when leaders focus on solving big problems, they become more conscious.

Exponential Theory: The Power of Thinking Big will examine a variety of companies that are seeking to solve big problems and have become more conscious than other companies focused on just profit. In return, these companies have grown beyond comprehension. Their leaders have their eyes on impacting a billion people and understand the importance of their role in the planet, in assisting in human rights, and in living up to a massive purpose that solves an equally big problem.

Many of these companies serve two-and three-sided businesses models, leveraging platforms benefiting many different stakeholders. The platforms accelerate growth beyond models with fixed assets or companies that serve only one customer. As companies begin to think systemically, their decision criteria change quickly. The democratization of industries has invited the masses to the party and given a voice to the previously silenced. Exponential theory forces companies that want to serve the masses to become more conscious or die.

When people work on projects that focus on impacting a billion people, they are forced to think about the system rather than just satisfying one group of customers. At this level, entrepreneurs and innovators are starting to focus on universal problems and change the way the system works. Therefore, these future Goliaths are starting to do the right thing, even when no one is looking. The pressure to do so may be that today leaders and companies are under the microscope.

Thinking big, starts with our planet, then with every human, animal, and living thing in the world. The survivability, sustainability and thrivability relies on future leaders to step up to the challenge. This book will share stories of how individuals and small groups of people that are thinking big are creating most of the change we see in the world. Currently our world is a giant system out of harmony, and we can do better. Ignoring the problems of others outside of our circle is no longer possible. Growing our circle of concern will start to help us solve bigger problems.

Whether we know it or not, the planet, oceans, land, fresh water, humans, animals, biodiversity, and the entire ecosystem needs to be a stakeholder in our decisions. If we are ignorant to doing the right thing for each of these stakeholders, it will have repercussions for us sharing the same ecosystem. For far too long, we have made decisions for the short-term and decisions to benefit just a few. Our future responsibility is protecting all these elements. Thinking small does not serve us well.

An early example of this short-sighted leadership is when gray wolves were exterminated from the Greater Yellowstone Ecosystem, as they were predators and caused trouble for nearby ranchers' herds. By 1926, gray wolves were completely eradicated. The removal directly caused an increase in the elk population, which devastated the ecosystem by disproportionately eating young trees and plants. This resulted in the demise of many trees, plants, birds and beavers turning the land into a barren forest. The glory of Yellowstone was nearly completely lost.

The reintroduction of wolves proves that by thinning the weak and sick animals, wolves create more resilient Elk herds. As Chris Wilmer's, a wildlife ecologist at the University of California, Santa Cruz, says, "Elk are not starving to death anymore." One decision led to a complete decimation of one of the largest wilderness ecosystems in the world.[12] Nature has a way of finding balance, until humans intervene. Similarly, the overfishing of our oceans has thrown the ocean ecosystem out of balance. Simply put, if our oceans die, we die. The systemic issues of overfishing have the potential to kill the planet.[13] Exponential theory seeks to understand and explain the interconnected relationships between all these seemingly disparate systems to find conscious solutions that benefit everyone in the ecosystem.

The Rhodium Rule

As leaders seek to leverage technology, they must start to become aware of the impact on other parts of the ecosystem. This leads to introducing a new rule in leadership:

The Rhodium Rule:

"Think about the entire ecosystem."

Dating back to before biblical times, the Golden Rule was a moral rule to "Treat others the way you want to be treated yourself." Fast forward to today, current culture would demand the Platinum Rule which states, "Treat people the way they want to be treated." Exponential theory introduces the Rhodium Rule, "Think about the entire ecosystem." Rhodium is the most expensive metal in the world and can be found in platinum, so Rhodium reinforces the Platinum Rule, yet introduces a value that aligns all the powers of exponential theory in a simple way.

THE **GOLDEN** RULE	THE **PLATINUM** RULE	THE **RHODIUM** RULE
99	99	99
Treat others the way **you want to be treated** yourself.	Treat people the way **they want to be treated**.	Think about the **entire ecosystem**.
66	66	66

Great innovators and entrepreneurs challenge the boundaries of many problems using the scientific method-ask questions, research, conduct a hypothesis, test a hypothesis by doing an experiment, analyze the data, draw a conclusion, and report the results. Was the hypothesis correct?

Exponential theory challenges every problem in a systematic way. Successful leaders focus on big ideas and small bets, not small ideas and big bets. For far too long, companies have bet the farm pouring billions into research and development without any proof. There is a new way to create evidence-based change based on data, feedback, and customer growth.

We are currently in the biggest explosion of disruption, as technology continues to drastically change everything. Linear thinking leaders will be blindsided by the coming big thinking innovations built on an exponential trajectory. Many current leaders have fought in a zero-sum game, yet future leaders will need to seek to expand the pie for all the stakeholders. This is proof that we are moving from a fixed mindset to growth mindset, and from scarcity to abundance. This is happening now, not in the past or the future.

When humans embrace exponential theory, we can better explain how we move from a linear to a circular economy. This new approach will help us find how to infinitely recycle, use renewable energy, clean the oceans, protect animal ecosystems, proactively heal humans, protect human rights, and salvage the climate. Humans will use exponential theory to eliminate global poverty and starvation, eliminate war (nuclear or otherwise), and make economic crises obsolete by shifting one mindset at a time from scarcity to abundance. We can move from healthcare (reactive) to wellness care (proactive) and potentially eradicate disease entirely through genetic engineering and new biotech solutions to solve nearly every medical issue. We are on the verge of massive breakthroughs nearly every day.

One thing is clear, we must begin to think about the long term, about future generations, for our planet to survive. The Iroquois people have a principle that decisions should be made with the next seven generations in mind.[14] This is something we should consider as we continue to deplete our natural capital for the short-term benefit of globalization focused solely on production and consumption; an unsustainable practice for a planet that has finite resources. We live on a spinning ball rotating around a Sun with clearly defined edges and limitations. Once we use the resources inside that spinning ball, they are gone. So, the use of coal, gas, and other unsustainable resources are limited, and we must shift towards renewable sources sooner than later. Regardless, we will need to shift away as they will eventually run out.

Exponential theory invokes optimism to deal with all these issues and reimagine a new future. Big thinkers have an opportunity to embrace this optimistic accelerated change en route to creating massive transformation like global cooperation, systemic racism reforms, and massive climate change reversal. The next generation must reimagine how we do just about everything, as the past has only led us here as we sit in a wasteland of excess and mass inequities.

Big thinkers know that no matter how complicated the problem, that the problems are solvable. The impact of an individual or a small group of focused people is incredible, nearly every story in this book highlights a small group of people that solved a big problem. Leaders will think differently after completing this book: first, by recognizing the needed change around us, removing our own limitations, and implementing exponential theory to find local and global solutions alike. The goal of this book is to create an army of leaders working to solve the biggest challenges leveraging exponential theory.

The Power of Thinking Big

With digitization and the resultant Fourth Industrial Revolution merging physical, digital, and biological worlds, dozens of exponential technologies have emerged and accelerated to center stage. The power of thinking big is here. For example, artificial intelligence (AI) combined with other exponential technologies—like the internet of things (IoT), 3D printing, robotics, or genetic engineering-create a multiplying effect. As technology gets exponentially more powerful, humans will start to see the world completely reinvented.

Technologies are helping us meet our basic needs and will continue to drive down the cost of housing, food, clothing, security, transportation, and communication. Meanwhile, automation and robots will one day care for us in ways previously unimaginable. The rising connected, autonomous, sharing, and electric economies will make the world less expensive. Energy will be abundant, local, and nearly free as the Sun gives the Earth more power in a single hour than we need all year.[15] Inevitably, everybody could potentially wear contact lenses with layers of augmented or mixed reality, controlled by our bio-implanted brain-computer interface. The future will be unapologetically different, and technology will play a role in nearly every part of our lives. Although technology is starting to disappear into the background, access to it continues to be democratized, abundant, and more equitable.

As a result of this marriage between humans and exponential technology, life will improve for nearly everyone on the planet. People will have more time to spend with their children, families, and friends. We will work less, spending time on the pursuit of our purpose. Humans will spend more time on leisure and outdoor activities, increase their exercise, eat better, and obesity rates will drop as behavioral economists nudge habits and technology improves access and education for everyone. Spirituality will likely rise as people have more time to pursue their desires and seek community, meaning, and faith. Suicide rates will likely plummet as we learn how to rewire our brains, balance our hearts, and take care of our guts. We will reimagine the future of health. As humans gets healthier, morality and consciousness will become more important. The glass is half full. With knowledge and hopefully wisdom, ignorance can be overcome.

In the next ten years, technology will drive down cost as we move towards technical abundance. Time will become the social currency, there will be an influx of volunteerism, giving back, and rallying together leveraging exponential theory to solve wicked problems. Through the Black Lives Matter movement, we've seen how humans organize and mobilize at scale. Now the world must take action against a system set up to exploit differences as we should be celebrating them. The ALS ice-bucket challenge raised over two hundred million dollars for research and awareness of the disease. Entire states and countries have banished plastic straws to help protect sea turtles. Movements around reducing, reusing, and recycling are starting to make a difference.

The power of thinking big has always been there. Fred Smith, the founder of FedEx, wrote a college term paper at Yale that got a "C."[16] The idea was to create overnight delivery through a hub and spoke business model moving every piece of mail through Memphis in the middle of the night. In April 1973, this business was launched with 14 small aircraft from Memphis International Airport, FedEx delivered 186 packages to 25 U.S. cities from Rochester, New York, to Miami, Florida that night. The rest is history. That's the power of thinking big.

Similarly, in 1951, John Bogle wrote his senior thesis at Princeton that eventually led to the launch of Vanguard, offering no-load low-cost mutual funds and index funds that have democratized investing for small investors and created one of the world's largest fund management companies with over $7 trillion in assets.[17] Each of these ideas relied on thinking big. Each idea had critics focused on the short-term, yet over time each of these companies have changed its respective industries.

Socially conscious companies are creating incredible movements to solve the world's biggest issues. For example, companies like Plastic Bank, which created Social Plastic, a social currency of recycled ocean plastic that major companies buy and reuse for their products, have created a sustainable circular economy solution.[18] These ideas will continue to scale and gain momentum as the world becomes more conscious about our usage of plastic. Then there is Source (formerly Zero Mass Water), which creates clean filtered drinking water from solar cells, pulling water out of thin air.[19] This idea has the potential to solve healthy drinking water everywhere in the world. With this technology, water becomes abundant.

Even larger companies like Patagonia have made a more conscious effort to go to 64% recycled materials and launch Worn Wear, recycling over 130,000 pieces of clothing. This in response to the clothing industry contributing 10% of the pollution driving climate change.[20] Pandora, the global jewelry retailer has chosen to stop selling mined diamonds due to prohibitive cost, human rights issues, and sustainability.[21] Finally, Tony's Chocolonely is on a mission to eliminate slavery in the chocolate industry by providing slave-free chocolates and challenging the entire chocolate industry to do the same.[22] There will be many more companies like these making a huge impact on the future. These are just more examples of exponential theory as a small group of people are able to impact entire industries.

The speed of change will require lifelong learning as career and companies' lifespan continue to shrink. Leaders will start to collectively work together to solve nearly every problem humankind faces. Advancements in education technology (EdTech) will have both kids and adults learning at a pace never seen before. EdTech startups are bringing new ways to learn, leveraging each student's preferred modality, while also giving access to the best teachers in the world. New access to art technology will create another renaissance, like NFT's (non-fungible tokens) which have created a new form of digital art that verifies ownership on a blockchain. A relatively unknown artist @Beeple, sold a digital version of "Everyday's—the first 5,000 days," at Christie's Auction for $69 million.[23] This is an example of how we still create scarcity in an abundant economy. Regardless, Maslow's Hierarchy will be heavy at the top, as we shift from scarcity to abundance.

Because of digitization, leaders are on the cusp of some major breakthroughs. This book will guide us through these changes with a collection of stories about some of the most dominant companies and leaders on the planet. The ten ways of thinking big include: Embracing the VUCA World, Thinking Exponentially, Digitizing the Model, Becoming a Tech Company, Finding the Massive Transformative Purpose, Launching Disruption, Leveraging the Viral Loop, Playing the Long Game, Executing the MVP, and Accelerating Innovation. With the Great Reset and these powerful ideas, leaders can begin reimagining their purpose, impact, and future solutions to nearly everything that plagues us. Leaders will be able to reimagine the future. A future in which big thinkers will thrive.

Imagination—the human's sixth sense—will empower leaders to envision a new future that will look nothing like our world does now. What we dream up, we will build. What we focus on, we will become. To think is to create, and what we resist persists. There is no time but now. Make sure to think big. Let's get started.

REFLECTION

To think is to create. How we spend our days is how we spend our lives. Focusing on personal habits and putting in the work will help us reach our goals. In Exponential Theory we will create the life we focus on.

- With everything on your mind written down, now schedule everything that is important to you over the next six weeks. Then, keep everything else on a backlog.
- If you are to be an exponential leader, are you spending your time on exponential activities?
- Do you practice the Golden Rule or the Platinum Rule?
- How are you going to implement the Rhodium Rule?
- How will you move from scarcity to abundance?

Chapter 2.

Embracing the VUCA World

"It is not the strongest species that survive, nor the most intelligent, but the ones most responsive to change."
—Charles Darwin

The VUCA world

The United States Army and its leaders were troubled: in 1987, the Cold War imploded in Afghanistan into a theater of disillusionment. Fueled by the opposing USSR's desire to conquer the Afghan nation and spread communism, Afghanistan was figuratively torn in two and the thirteen-year civil war that ensued claimed more than 1.5 million lives.[24] Despite the death toll, neither the Soviet Army nor the U.S.-backed mujahideen was closer to victory. The situation was so out of control that the U.S. Army had to come up with a new term to describe it: VUCA.

- Volatility: a tendency to change quickly and unpredictably.
- Uncertainty: doubt, with no certainty.
- Complexity: the multiple forces compounding an issue; the confusion inhibiting an organization.
- Ambiguity: the loss of reality; disconnection to cause-and-effect.

The volatility in Afghanistan required military leaders to create a shared vision that extended beyond the immediate chaos into the future of what the country could be. During times of uncertainty, leaders sought new levels of understanding of the Afghan people and their needs in order to properly assess the situation and move forward. This meant better listening, empathy, and accepting critical feedback from those most affected by the civil war. The complexity of the war expanded leaders' horizons by forcing them to rethink aspects they might previously have ignored, like the difficult combat terrain or the large number of civilians in between them and the enemy. Leaders needed to create clarity in the complexity. Lastly, ambiguity forced military leaders to be agile and flexible, so that they could adapt to the unpredictable nature of the changing war. The four facets of VUCA guide military and exponential leaders alike by focusing on traits necessary for success in today's world.

Leaders can use the VUCA mental model to address the changing landscape of the digital world, and better understand the implications of their decisions. To plan for the volatile, uncertain, complex, and ambiguous landscape of the digital world, we adopt a new VUCA mental model—to seek vision, understanding, clarity, and agility.[25]

With the new VUCA mental model, leaders seek:

- Vision: establish a clear massive transformative purpose and . . .
- Understanding: invoke continuous communication, empathy, and active listening, with an emphasis on diversity and data to . . .
- Clarity: simplify, create expectations, and educate as we seek to . . .
- Agility: experiment, fail, learn, and repeat.

Using VUCA to identify and solve a problem is the first step in thinking big and leveraging exponential theory. Innovation, after all, is the process of solving problems and/or incrementally improving what already exists. When there's a problem, humans innovate. When there is an opportunity to improve something, we innovate. Innovation accelerates life. Innovation demands new leadership. Leaders need to push into the unknown-learning, making mistakes, challenging the status quo, being lean, iterative and agile, creating the needed change in the world. This is an open call for the new VUCA Leadership. Leaders that move at light speed. Leaders that think big. Leaders who can solve big problems.

The Accelerating Speed of Innovation

In 3000 BC in Egypt, people began to write on papyrus, a reed growing on the banks of the Nile River.[26] This allowed people to communicate beyond the moment and resulted in the first known writings outside of carvings on clay and stone (an impractical way to communicate).

In 1440, Johannes Gutenberg created the printing press, enabling printed information to circulate across borders and be distributed to the masses. The increased access to knowledge eventually pulled people out of the dark ages into a world of innovation. People began to communicate through paper, literacy grew, and revolutionary ideas were shared throughout the world.

In the 19th century, people were tired of living in the dark. First, John D. Rockefeller's wealth soared to the richest man of his time as he nearly controlled the supply of kerosene, a better illuminant used in lamps at night. Then Thomas Edison created the lightbulb for the masses so that people could communicate, read, and write during the night hours. The lightbulb became the symbol of innovation.

During that time, global transportation was also evolving rapidly: people began using passenger trains in Liverpool, England in 1830.[27] These were improved upon when Karl Benz invented the first combustion engine car in 1886 in Stuttgart, Germany.[28] JP Morgan's financing and Andrew Carnegie's near monopoly on steel led to railroads western expansion and created the first industrial revolution. Jay Gould and Cornelius Vanderbilt cornered the railroads, which could be considered the internet of their time. Then, flight became a possibility in 1903 when the Wright brothers flew the first airplane in Kittyhawk, North Carolina. Each invention facilitated and expedited the movement of people and goods. At the same time, Alexander Graham Bell's telephone was gaining popularity, improving upon Edison's telegraph, and the world was connected for the first time.

One might say the late 1800s and early 1900s was the golden age of the inventor, if they did not live in our time. The telephone line eventually brought us data as AOL brought us online with over 6 billion CD's (Compact Disc) that marketed their service in the mid-90's with the mystical sound of dial up connecting to somewhere else in a far-off place. From there, speeds have rapidly accelerated. Each progressive technology sped up life, connected us to more information, people, and opportunities. We have been headed towards information overload for a long time.

Presently, leaders are prototyping hyperloops that travel at 760 miles per hour (mph) making a trip from Los Angeles to San Francisco possible in thirty-five minutes.[29] The SpaceX shuttle could take passengers from New York to Shanghai in less than forty minutes at speeds up to 16,700 mph moving on the edges of our atmosphere.[30] Finally, for short trips, we will use flying cars, flying robots, and passenger drones that will one day whisk passengers and deliveries of everything imaginable. A trip from Orange County to Burbank in less than 15 minutes, dodging hour-long commuter traffic jams. Interestingly, there's a simultaneous resurgence in bicycling and other green, formerly outdated transportation. Who would've thought that roller blades, skateboards, and scooters (now electric) would make a comeback? Since building the first railroads, and then interstate highways, ports and airports, humans have reimagined transportation with many innovative solutions. These solutions have created more practical ways to get from point A to point B, everything from the last mile to space travel.

While innovation is as old as the wheel itself, the difference now is that we have dramatically increased our ability to innovate. We now have infinite ways to innovate. We have infinite information at our fingertips. We can use design thinking to create new emerging technologies quickly. We can study nature and how it has survived and thrived for 3.8 billion years (a process called biomimicry) and replicate its best ideas to solve some of the world's most challenging problems. We can use the work of Russian innovator Genrich Altshuller's TRIZ (the Theory of Inventive Problem Solving) after studying hundreds of thousands of patents, he found 1,500 basic problems and 40 universal answers to solve them all. Finally, we can use systems thinking to innovate the whole rather than just the parts.

Exponential theory solves much more complex problems building on the innovative methods that have gotten us here. Innovation can be learned, and creativity can be trained. Thus, with thinking big, exponential theory and the coming disruption, we must completely reimagine the future, even questioning the evolutionary instincts that are hardwired in humans.

The Hardwired Brain

Innovation is literally hardwired into humans.

Human DNA has evolved over time and helps produce generations stronger than the previous ones, slowly adapting to the environment around it. Our immune systems develop antibodies to protect us from viruses and diseases. Yet, our brain is ten thousand years old and still seeking environmental signals to know if we should fight or flight or freeze so we don't get eaten by a lion on the savanna. Our amygdala, which controls this function, is a collection of cells located near the base of the brain and is our first environmental filter. Thus, our tool kit that our ancestry relied on still drives our subconscious.

Scientists who study epigenetics—how DNA expression changes over time without physically altering—understand that generational trauma affects human instincts. Humans know to run when a lion approaches, as fight or freeze are less effective. If the goal is preserving one's life, we inherently know this and relive the experience as a déjà vu over and over again subconsciously. The executive decision making of the prefrontal cortex is basically powered off. We repeat many of our actions until we can break the cycle by bypassing the amygdala's instinct.

The hardwired brain runs automatically. This is what Nobel Prize-winning psychologist and economist Daniel Kahneman describes as two separate systems of mental processing in his book *Thinking Fast and Slow*. System One is fast, unconscious, effortless, and automatic. System One makes quick decisions, which are often mental shortcuts we've created through evolution, or thinking we've been in the situation before. System Two, however, is slow, deliberate, conscious, effortful, and controlled.[31] The key to innovation is using System Two more effectively through mental models, philosophy, reading, case studies, and learning how others handle the situation. If System One takes over in a crisis, we have fewer options to respond. There is a lack of creativity when the brain is caught in a state of trauma, a paradox of choice, analysis paralysis, and/or the left-brain analytical mode has taken over automatically.

At the same time, trauma, friction, and conflict force innovation. For example, the coronavirus pandemic may be the biggest digital transformation in history, outperforming any other long-term corporate digital transformation initiative in just a few months. The pandemic forced companies to transform due to organizational stress, and they quickly shifted to remote working, video conferencing, digital sales, and companies sought technology solutions for nearly everything. Crisis often invigorates innovation.

Crisis creates Opportunity

I n 1977, Citibank invested hundreds of millions in ATM technology across New York City. Yet no one used them until the blizzard of 1978 when multiple feet of snow shut down the city.[32] Prior to this, people would cash their checks at the supermarket. But when the supermarkets ran out of cash, only then did people find their way to ATMs. Today, ATMs are widely used to withdraw money around the world; but they had to break through the norm to do it.

Unfortunately, most companies, organizations, and social institutions act as a brain in System One. It gets used to doing something one way and makes it as efficient as possible. It doesn't want to change, adapt, or innovate. In fact, it fights change just like the System One brain would, by killing new ideas and protecting the status quo. The bureaucracy has one way to do something, even if common sense would identify that it is not working. A complex system will fight change at all costs.

This is why change is so difficult to achieve. New ideas are killed in the boardroom, executive teams remain non-diverse, and peaceful protestors get tear gassed. The only time change happens rapidly is when the rubber band has been pulled so far and the world snaps back to head in another direction after changing too fast. We've seen this in American presidential candidates over the last couple decades, with extreme change and instability from one President to the next. This is the same reason many people have to have a heart attack to change their diet; the body is crying for changes to be made.

If companies, organizations, and social institutions were truly System Two—deliberate, self-aware, and logical—then new ideas, diversity, and even protestors would be embraced. We would seek diversity, embrace others with different opinions, and continuously learn, adapting to new information. We would seek out learning opportunities from other companies, in other industries, and avoid the same pitfalls. Unfortunately, this is not the case. In the VUCA world, those who are not conscious, mindful, or purposeful will be disrupted. The world demands people do the right thing, yet the right thing may be just what the majority views is the right thing. With digitization comes transparency as everything is video-taped, recorded, emailed, and shared in some way or another. Doing the right thing when no one is looking is very important to future leadership, or the rubber band will snap leaders in a new direction. The speed of the world is putting more pressure and stress on companies, organizations, and social institutions than ever before as we all shift from the linear growth to the exponential curve.

REFLECTION

It's not what happens to you, it's how you respond. The VUCA world is Volatile, Uncertain, Complex and Ambiguous. Responding to challenges in this environment requires Vision, Understanding, Clarity and Agility.

- What's your vision personally? Professionally? Organizationally?
- How often do you seek to understand, before responding?
- What parts of your life are very clear, and which parts do you need to seek clarity on?
- How agile are you when unexpected things happen?
- How can you innovate yourself?

Chapter 3.

Thinking Exponentially

"The greatest shortcoming of the human race is our inability
to understand the exponential function."
—**Albert Allen Bartlett, Professor**

The First Exponential Organization

One of the top Google searches for Bill Gates is, "Did Bill Gates invent the internet?"

No, Bill Gates did not invent the internet. Neither did Al Gore. ARPANET officially created the first computer connection in 1969. Later, Tim-Berners Lee was responsible for commercializing the internet with the world wide web. This paved the way for companies like Facebook, Skype, and Twitter to communicate in new ways.

However, as many of the early computer companies focused on hardware, Bill Gates focused on building the applications that would go inside all the hardware—the software. In 1975, Bill Gates and Paul Allen founded a computer software company called Microsoft and proclaimed that they would put a computer on every desk in every home.[33] At the time, people thought that Gates and Allen were out of their minds. It was difficult for the average person to see why they would need a computer at work, let alone a computer in every home. In 1975, the computer was a complex functioning system that only major companies invested in.

Gates and Allen weren't crazy, though—they saw a future that many others could not. They knew that computers were one of many exponential technologies that would inevitably change the world. These exponential technologies were the catalyst for accelerated change and disruption. Gates and Allen were going to be the first surfers on the exponential growth wave to become one of the largest companies in the world-so influential Gates still gets mistaken for the guy who invented the internet.

> *"Most people overestimate what they can do in one year and underestimate what they can do in ten years."*
> **—Bill Gates**

Microsoft created Microsoft-Disk Operating System (MS—DOS). This operating system—the precursor to Windows—standardized how individuals would use the personal computer. Computers began taking over desks in offices and soon after, as predicted, reached homes. These computers ran on MS—DOS and later Microsoft Windows, run largely by a floppy disk the user had to shove into the disc drive. Soon, Microsoft Office had the business world running on Word, Excel, PowerPoint, and Outlook. Internet Explorer had nearly everyone on the web. Microsoft was one of the first companies to grow exponentially.

Microsoft became the largest software company
in the world.

Bill Gates (at the time) became the richest man
in the world.

Gates and Allen provided millions of people and businesses with an exponential tool. Productivity skyrocketed as more and more tasks became digitized. The Microsoft Office software suite became standard operating technology for much of corporate America and the world. Microsoft launched Xbox in 2001 in response to the Sony PlayStation amid concerns it was a threat to the personal computer. Microsoft has remained relevant with the purchases of Skype,[34] LinkedIn,[35] GitHub,[36] Minecraft, and the rollout of Office 365 powering their move to the cloud.

Currently, five Exponential Organizations (ExOs) have risen to the top of the technology world in the western hemisphere and have become global brands in the process: Facebook, Apple, Google (Alphabet Inc.), Microsoft, and Amazon. Globally, people use or interact with these companies in some way every day. Salim Ismail first outlined ExOs in his book *Exponential Organizations* when he noticed similarities between companies that grew 10x, Unicorns (startups with $1 billion-dollar valuations), and the leading technology companies in the world.[37] As we dive deeper into exponential theory, we will examine these ExOs more closely.

In his work, Salim Ismail defined ExOs as companies that are ten times larger than peer companies, with four or more specific internal or external attributes (as defined below), and a Massive Transformative Purpose (MTP). The MTP functions as the "why," the motivation for why a company operates. Simon Sinek has made a living helping people think about their why. This philosophy is driving purpose-driven growth companies and a movement towards Environmental, Societal, and Governmental (ESG) companies making an impact. An MTP often describes the ExOs vision for a better future for the industry, the community, and the world at large.

From Salim Ismail's book *Exponential Organizations*, here are the five internal and five external attributes of an exponential organization using the acronyms IDEAS and SCALE.[38]

Internal (IDEAS):

- Interfaces: ExOs have very customized processes for how they interface with customers and other organizations.
- Dashboards: A real-time, adaptable dashboard with all essential company and employee metrics, accessible to everyone in the organization.

- Experimentation: Implementation of the Lean Startup methodology of testing assumptions and constantly experimenting with controlled risks.
- Autonomy: Self-organizing, multidisciplinary teams operating with decentralized authority.
- Social Technologies: Social technologies, or collaborative technologies, allow organizations to manage real-time communication among all employees.

External (SCALE):
- Staff on Demand: Minimize full-time staff and outsource tasks. Uber uses staff on demand when they incentivize drivers to go online during busy times.
- Community and Crowd: If we build communities and we do things in public, we don't have to find the right people—they find us.
- Algorithms: ExOs leverage data and algorithms to scale in ways that were not possible just five or ten years ago.
- Leveraged Assets: Hold on to what's critical. Outsource everything else. Access not ownership.
- Engagement: Enabling collaborative human behavior (social behavior) to engineer the results we want from our community.

Leaders use these internal and external attributes to create a compounding effect, where change accelerates, producing more efficient processes, strategies, technologies, and organizations. For example, with the compounding effect, a negligible improvement can be dramatic over time. A 1% improvement everyday compounds into a 37x improvement after one year. IDEAS and SCALE pay off in the long run, though in the short term, none of these attributes are likely to make a noticeable difference. Using these attributes, ExOs like Facebook, Apple, Google (Alphabet Inc.), Microsoft, and Amazon have grown to be very BIG companies, with influence larger than governments. New companies like Uber, Airbnb, Netflix and others leverage these principles to grow faster than other companies, taking over their industries in a short period of time. They are likely to be the giant companies of tomorrow.

These ExOs have also created massive opportunities for employment beyond just their own employees, creating new economies of their own. For example, Amazon reported that it employed more than 1.2 million employees worldwide in 2020, yet the company also enables employment for nearly two million more people through the third-party marketplace and logistics network.[39]

Apple, Google (Alphabet Inc.), Microsoft, and Amazon have all surpassed a trillion-dollar market capitalization and continue to grow regardless of the external economic climate.

$1,000,000,000,000

To better understand exponential growth, here's a short story. A little girl is negotiating her allowance with her parents. "Just pay me a penny and double my pay every week." Sounds easy enough. At first glance, this sounds like a great deal.

By week four, she's only making eight cents a week. Her parents still feel like it's a good deal. After two months, she's making $2.56 a week. In six months, she's making $335,544.32 a week, and after one year, her earnings are equal to the GDP of the United States of America. She accepts Venmo, PayPal, or Apple Pay.

Exponential growth is a game changer.

This is why traditional companies are not able to compete with exponential companies.

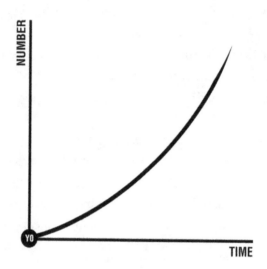

Leveraging the power of exponential change makes linear change obsolete. Take a linear counting sequence: 1, 2, 3, 4, 5, 6, 7, 8, 9, 10, 11, 12 . . . Now consider an exponential sequence: 1, 2, 4, 8, 16, 32, 64, 128, 256, 512, 1,024, 2,048 . . . Exponential growth leaves linear growth in the dust before it can count to four, doubling the results.

So, it's foolish to try and do business on a linear trajectory moving forward. Innovation needs to be reimagined. Companies are unable to seek 10% incremental gains like before. Instead, companies must find 10x growth and improvements to avoid being irrelevant in the future. The telephone grew its user base on a linear trajectory. It took nearly fifty years to reach fifty-million people. The radio took thirty-eight years to reach fifty-million people. The TV only took twenty-two years to reach fifty-million people. Growing exponentially, the internet took just seven years, Facebook a mere three years, and as the technology compounded

Pokémon Go reached fifty million people in just nineteen days.[40] Speed continues to accelerate and is truly the main competitive advantage for a future filled with abundance.

Subsequently, the average life of a technology company is shrinking rapidly. Entrepreneurs aren't creating pop-up companies just yet, but they're not far from it. A recent study by global management consultancy McKinsey & Company found that the average life span of companies listed in Standard & Poor's 500 was sixty-one years in 1958. Today, it is less than fifteen years. McKinsey believes that in 2027, 75% of the companies currently quoted on the S&P 500 will have disappeared.[41] General Electric (GE) was the last original company removed from the Dow 30 in 2018.

This shift can best be explained by a few laws that decipher the move from a linear to an exponential world. Moore's Law, Keck's Law of Fiber, Metcalfe's Law of Networks, and Kurzweil's Law of Accelerating Returns provide a foundation to understand how big we really can think.

- Moore's Law (named after Gordon Moore, Intel co-founder) found that computing power doubles every eighteen months.[42]
- Donald Keck's Law of Fiber states that fiber optic cables—another exponential technology—have a power that doubles every nine months, twice as fast as computing power.[43]
- Robert Metcalfe's (co-inventor of Ethernet) Law states that networking power is squared with each user that joins a network, automatically creating exponential potential from the start.[44]

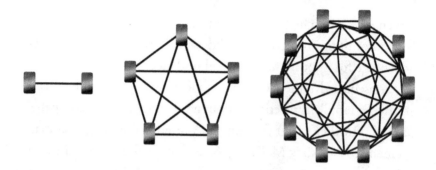

- Ray Kurzweil's Law of Accelerating Returns states that technology will leverage other technologies and constantly and automatically improve itself. Thus, technological progress is exponential. He writes, "So we won't experience 100 years of progress in the 21st century; it will be more like 20,000 years of progress. . . " [45]

These laws compound on one another, and technological processes will never slow down. The rate of change that people experience will become increasingly faster.

Now five billion people (and counting) have been added to the global network (Metcalfe's Law) and we've created a massive marketplace for growth through connectivity. Therefore, the human species is more connected than ever before, with access to more and more opportunities than ever before. The extraordinary increase in human connectivity is the fuel for the fire of exponential theory and disruption.

Mass access and connectivity have largely been enabled by personal internet devices like smartphones. With this robust computing power and instant access to information in our pockets, we are all tremendously empowered. Mass access has enabled people to organize, spurring powerful crowd-generated movements such as Occupy Wall Street, the Arab Spring, and Black Lives Matter.

These movements were empowered and organized by digital revolutions. One thing is clear: the power is shifting from the few to the masses. Even a group of investors banded together on Reddit's #WallStreetBets, drove the GameStop stock up 1,400% in a week, losing billions for a few hedge fund managers who were shorting the stock.[46] The global power of social media is chasing extreme opinions from the fringes of society to the center of controversy, exposing oppression and the need for equality and justice for all. The masses have the ability to think big, demand change, and now control the lever to create that change for themselves.

While technology begins to do most of the heavy lifting for routine and meaningless tasks, human energy is better utilized in finding creative solutions for the remaining issues. While mass access creates connectivity for every corner of our planet, humanity unites in an unprecedented way. Soon, many global crises surrender to the sustained wisdom of crowds, empathy, and big thinkers that dare solve nearly every problem humankind has identified.

Consequently, with mass access, both the volume of consumers and their expectations have grown exponentially. The number of products and services creates abundance for consumers. The market flips upside down from a scarcity economy to an abundant economy, one that centers on the concepts of "free" and "unlimited."

The Sharing Economy

The sharing economy creates abundance in nearly every industry. The sharing economy enables people to share just about anything such as cars, bikes, rooms, homes, desks, phones, clothes, shoes, purses, luggage, books, movies, games, boats, jet skis, RVs, quads, gardens, prom dresses, and everything imaginable that we once preferred to own.[47]

In the sharing economy, people can access more for less, which creates more individual discretionary income and freedom for every person on the planet. If we can pay a small fee to get rides across town with Uber or Lyft, why buy an expensive car, gas, oil, tires, maintenance, insurance, or a license plate and worry about parking? All of these industries will be disrupted as access over ownership is shifting society nearly overnight. This shift is a huge win for our planet, as resources become reusable, and we need less of them to satisfy the entire population. Digitization has enabled a whole new set of desires. The car is no longer the center of the universe for urban teenagers, and many are increasingly opting out of getting their driving license.

Digital technology has created a whole new spectrum of opportunities, and continues to lower the cost of other technologies, enabling billions to entertain, share, and connect from anywhere in the world. With an abundant digital economy, consumers are now able to consume more than ever before: better, cheaper, and faster. Consumers do not have to choose just two of these; rather, they are demanding all three. Technology has enabled better outcomes, for cheaper prices, and faster than ever before. So, to lead in the future, we must adopt both the mass access and sharing economy mindsets; thinking big enough to figure out how to provide access to all. Brands need to embrace the entire ecosystem to exist as product differentiation diminishes in a digital world and the choice of quality over quantity disappears. Abundance is about to change everything. Consumers are starting to understand they need less ownership and only a few access points.

Disruptive Technologies

In just over forty years since Gates and Allen plotted to put a computer in every home, the world has become massively digitized. Instead of a single computer in every house, there's a computer in every pocket, wrist, kitchen, bathroom, electronic device, and TV. The Internet of Things (IoT) will connect nearly everything in the future. In fact, it is predicted there will be 30 to 75 billion IoT connected devices by 2025.

Examples of this include artificial intelligence (AI) powered voice-activated bots in our homes; sensors that record our every move; drones that deliver packages; robots that automatically order groceries, and networks of autonomous vehicles at our disposal. All these exponential technologies have become reality thanks to digitization and disruption of the norm. Digital transformation has forced a new norm. The Emerging Technologies Stack shares a viewpoint of the technologies coming to market over the next 10-25 years. As we look out into the future, the timeline may shift, yet innovators are working on every one of these technologies and they all have implications for nearly every industry on this planet.

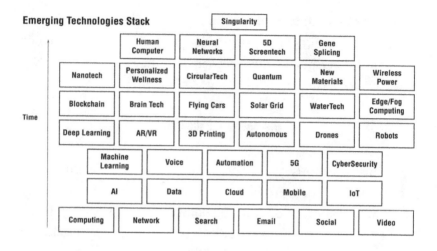

As Singularity University explains, "Exponential technologies are those which are rapidly accelerating, shaping major industries, and all aspects of our lives."[48] The foundations of exponential technologies are built on computing, networks, search, email, social, and video. The next layer that has accelerated change even more includes AI, data, cloud, mobile, and internet of things (IoT). All technologies that have become pervasive in this century. Thereafter, we move into science fiction with blockchain, augmented reality (AR), virtual reality (VR), 3D printing, autonomous cars, drones, and robotics. As new exponential technologies are invented, they begin to stack onto each other, building off the layer beneath it, and thus compounding both their power and impact. This continues to accelerate as each of these ideas (and more) are built on top of each other.

Digitization continues to change how we do everything. People take digital pictures and video of nearly everything and put them online. Arguments can be sorted out with a Google search. Everybody has access to somebody's Netflix account with infinite entertainment on demand. Amazon Prime has orders at your door in one hour. Grandma has an iPhone, and your youngest cousin just taught her how to use emojis and Snapchat. Your grandparents even use Facebook, and now order delivery meals through apps like Door Dash, Grub Hub and UberEATS.

Software as A Service

In 2008, Adobe sold boxes of their perpetual licensed design software (most notably Photoshop) to creative professionals through big-box retail channels like Circuit City and Best-Buy. In the last great recession, Adobe was hit hard as corporations stopped spending money to update those boxes of software. Adobe needed to reinvent itself. In 2011, Adobe moved away from their perpetual license software (buy a box), in favor of a cloud-based subscription model that moved all their products into a service bundle. Further digitizing their business model—moving in unison with Netflix, Google, Apple, and Amazon Web Services—ultimately changed how people buy everything: access over ownership. Unfortunately, perpetual licensed software recognized revenue immediately, while subscription revenue would be earned over time. This had a huge impact on Adobe's immediate earnings.

With no other option than to take a hit on their earnings and pivot, Adobe created the Creative Cloud. The cloud could store content, enable collaboration, work seamlessly, and provide access to all Adobe products. Adobe took on a "burn the boats" approach and eliminated the product option altogether, forcing their customers to purchase a service over a product. The goal was to expedite customer migration from an old model that was not working to a new model that would create a new digital company and new, more repeatable, predictable, scalable, and sustainable revenue streams.

Adobe had charged up to $1,800 for access to all its products in its perpetual licensing model but moved customers to the cloud for as little as fifty dollars a month for the same access. They even offered access to one product for nineteen dollars. Between 2011 and 2014, revenues dropped while subscriptions started to grow. By 2020, it had created over $13.4 billion in total revenue.[49]

This 10x growth was the result of Adobe's ability to think big and their commitment to a new digital model. Adobe's digital transformation was unprecedented, as other companies have not taken such divisive action. Their stock has responded with 10x gains, rewarding the investors moving to the digital model while demonetizing, dematerializing, and democratizing their software to the masses. Their customer base expanded, too: originally geared toward graphic designers, videographers, and professional marketers, Adobe customers now included Instagrammers, bloggers, and entrepreneurs. Adobe continued to acquire more tools and built out a suite of analytics, marketing, and graphic design tools catering to corporate clients through large licensing programs.

> *"We always had the right motivation, which is: How can we innovate at a faster pace? How can we aggressively acquire new customers and how can we continue to build a more predictable and recurring revenue stream?"*
> **—Shantanu Narayen,** Adobe CEO, on why they moved Adobe to the cloud[50]

It's clear with the Adobe story that disruption has drastically changed the business landscape. Companies like Enron, World-Com, and Lehman Brothers deconstructed, while Kodak, Borders, and Circuit City became irrelevant nearly overnight. Companies like General Electric (GE), Exxon Mobil, Proctor and Gamble (P&G), and DowDuPont are among the oldest companies on the New York Stock Exchange, yet they will be left behind if they do not address the disruption of the changing digital landscape in business right now.

The Disruption Framework

As we experience accelerating change, we simultaneously experience accelerating disruption. Disruption is the growing gap between linear and exponential change. Essentially, what goes up (change) must force something else to go down (disruption). As Newton's Third Law of Physics states, for every action, there is an equal but opposite reaction. Change is the wave that carries a positive impact to shore. Disruption is what is left in the wake.

To better explain disruption, Peter Diamandis and Steven Kotler created the 6Ds framework to explain the various stages of companies' disruption.[51] An important part of innovation is the self-awareness of where a company stands compared to the competition within our own industry, parallel industries, substitute industries, or alternative industries, particularly within the disruptive process. For example, hoteliers need to look beyond their direct competitor to recognize the disruption (rooms booked, customers lost) that Airbnb is waging against them, and how they will need to pivot their business models to survive.

> *"The 6Ds are a chain reaction of technological progression, a road map of rapid development that always leads to enormous upheaval and opportunity."* [52]
> **—Peter Diamandis and Steven Kotler**

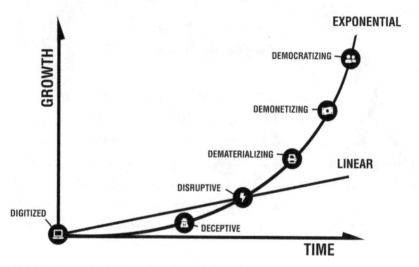

Original image adapted from Peter Diamandis and Steve Kotler's 6 D's of Disruption.

The six stages of disruption are:

Stage 1: Digitize

Once something becomes digitized, it gains the ability to be exponential. Digitization is the prerequisite for all change in the last twenty years. It is also the fundamental reason why we have seen such transformative change in nearly every industry. All industries are in some stage of digitization.

Stage 2: Deceptive

When technologies are deceptive, they may appear to be very slow in the early stages. For example, 3D printing has been around for nearly three decades, but only within the last five years has the technology been adopted en masse. 3D printing is now impacting expected industries—such as manufacturing and supply chain— but also automobiles, homes, household goods, food, clothes, and even space. For example, Made in Space created a 3D printer for non-gravity use,[53] saving millions in duplicate parts for the International Space Station.

Stage 3: Disruptive

When technology hits the disruptive stage, it reaches a point where the change is evident to society. This is where the exponential curve surpasses the linear growth, and change starts to make an impact beyond the industry. Music streaming subscriptions skyrocketed when Spotify reached the disruptive stage, while album sales plummeted on iTunes, creating Apple Music to respond and pivot to a subscription model.

Stage 4: Dematerialize

Once a technology is making an impact, the technology soon dematerializes. This means that in the span of just years, several technologies dematerialize into one small technology. The iPhone has over two million apps and counting[54], turning your phone into the ultimate multifunction tool that you can fit in your pocket. The TV, laptop, flashlight, radio, camera, and alarm clock can now all be found on a smartphone, making TV's and laptop sales decline and flashlights, radios, cameras, and alarm clocks nearly obsolete. The market simply disappeared.

Stage 5: Demonetization

Demonetization is next, and the technology is free or nearly free. Tesla is starting to demonetize the car, bringing the cost of an electric vehicle down with the Model 3 so the masses can afford it. After launching, over 450,000 people deposited money on the future car and as they delivered on these models the stock soared. Tesla is leveraging exponential battery technologies to drive costs down. The battery eliminates gas altogether and lowers demands for gas and oil, upending the traditional oil-producing super-powers and gas-guzzling combustion engine manufacturers. Tesla owners see a significant decrease in how much it costs to own, maintain, and operate a car. Soon Tesla could deploy an upgrade to their software and create the first fleet of fully autonomous revenue generating owners, further lowering the cost of ownership. This will further demonetize car ownership as Tesla car will begin to creating a new profit center for owners.

Stage 6: Democratize

Finally, democratization comes when technology spreads across the world, and becomes available to anyone and everyone. Arguably, as the internet has democratized, Wi-Fi is considered a basic right, even more so than running water in many parts of the world. Globally, McDonald's and Starbucks offer free Wi-Fi and plugs for electricity in their restaurants and cafes. With the internet and a smartphone, nearly everybody has the same access to the platforms and communication capabilities. As the economic differences between rich and poor have increased considerably, yet the lifestyle gap has simultaneously decreased, as both billionaires and homeless people seek the same Wi-Fi signals.

ExOs and *The Invincible Company*, as defined by Alex Oster-walder in his new book with that name, view disruption as an opportunity.[55] ExOs constantly reinvent themselves, compete on superior business models, and often transcend industry boundaries. This way, they are agile and less likely to get washed away by a disruption in their industry or another. Lean, iterative, and agile processes allow these new companies to respond quickly to changes in the marketplace.

The "too big to fail" principle that spared large companies in the past is not foolproof protection anymore. Just because a company's death poses a systemic risk to the global economy doesn't mean that it won't get swallowed by an ExO from another industry. The increase of mergers and acquisitions during the past few decades underscores the fact that large enterprises remain quite vulnerable. Large companies are acquiring competitors and disruptors to maintain growth, eliminate disruption, reduce inefficiencies, while hopefully gaining productivity, and speed.

Thinking big—like putting a computer in every home—is something that Microsoft and Bill Gates were able to do in the 1970s and 80s, fully realizing the exponential curve in the 1990s and beyond as they opened markets globally in nearly every country in the world. This can be replicated on an individual level by adopting the exponential theory, recognizing the laws of digital technology and the impact of mass access while understanding the many stages of the 6Ds of disruption. Previously, it took generations for companies to make the same impact that other companies are now making in a single year. Leaders now understand that they must either disrupt or be disrupted.

REFLECTION

We are always right. Salim Ismail identified 10 attributes of an Exponential Organization (ExO). Five internal attributes (IDEAS) are Interfaces, Dashboards, Experimentation, Autonomy, and Social Technologies. Five external attributes (SCALE) include Staff on Demand, Community and Crowd, Algorithms, Leveraged Assets, and Engagement.

- What attributes of an ExO does your organization already do?
- What attributes can you add to your organization?
- What exponential technologies can help your company change your business model?
- Consider the 6 Ds (Digitization, Deception, Disruption, Dematerialization, Demonetization, Democratization). What stage is your company in? Your industry?
- Using the emerging tech stack will help visualize the path to singularity. What technologies do you recognize?
- Which ones can you envision in your future?

Chapter 4

Digitizing the Model

"Technology is exponential, yet humans are linear."
—Gerd Leonhard, Futurist

Death to Blockbuster!—A Netflix Original

In 2004, the home video rental company Blockbuster was in almost every neighborhood in nearly every city. They offered the entire movie theater experience to be delivered into the home: video rentals, tubs of microwave buttered popcorn, rows of Twizzlers and Milk Duds at the checkout, and an ice chest full of ice-cold Coca-Cola sodas to go. Late fees, however, were exorbitant, and checkout lines were often long. If you couldn't go to the movie theater, Blockbuster was the place to be on a Friday or Saturday night.

Then, along came Redbox. Redbox's digital business model was simple: digital self-serve vending kiosks that loaned out DVDs, Blu-Rays, and the latest PS4 or Xbox video games. Redbox digitized the video store and dematerialized Blockbuster into a computer the size of a vending machine. Bulky VHS tapes used by video rental stores quickly became DVDs and Blu-Rays, which shrunk the amount of space needed to distribute videos to consumers.

Consider the extra expenses of Blockbuster that Redbox was able to shed: management, hourly staff, building rent, heating, air conditioning, lighting, promotions, printing, theft, damaged goods, and more. Redbox was significantly leaner and more agile without all the overhead expenses of Blockbuster. This is the power of dematerialization.

Without all the overhead, Redbox could turn a profit and still charge far less than Blockbuster, in addition to doing away with late fees. For customers, this was a no brainer: Who needs late fees in a world of abundance? This is the power of demonetization.

What once took up a whole storefront in a strip mall now fit into the size of a vending machine, perfectly placed outside every

McDonald's and Walgreens across the United States.[56] This is the power of democratization.

Then came Netflix, and Redbox's disruption quickly became obsolete.

Redbox, and whatever was left of Blockbuster, was swiftly decimated by the new digital service of Netflix, which took digitization a step further. Instead of vending machines, Netflix started with a website and home delivery, bypassing Blockbuster's high rent retail location and Redbox's vending empire. This idea was so brilliant that the website and home delivery model continues to disrupt many other industries today.

In the early days of Netflix, customers selected their movies by adding them to a queue of favorite movies online, and consumers were mailed the highest-ranked video that was available. Then, they were mailed another movie every time they returned their last rental. It was not instant, but it was significantly cheaper and engaging to consumers as the movies were continually mailed out whenever the previous one was returned. Then, Netflix disrupted itself by rolling out its current business model-a digital subscription model and shifted the video rental market completely online. At the same time shifted movies from a business built on scarcity to a business built on abundance.

Blockbuster operated in a scarcity market. Go back to Friday night in 2004, when a customer wanted to watch the new hot movie, like *Napoleon Dynamite*, *Crash*, or *The Notebook*. The neighborhood video rental store only had four copies, so customers would have to get there fast in order to get one. In a scarcity market, Blockbuster needed the video back to re-rent it and make more money from it. If it was not returned, they made up for that lost revenue with ridiculous late fees. If the movie slipped under your car seat and you found it a month later, you got slapped with a $100+ fee and could not rent another video until it was paid. Be kind, rewind! You were even penalized a $1 fee to rewind your video. At the height in 2004, there were 9,094 Blockbuster stores, now there is only one remaining Blockbuster franchise store in Bend, Oregon.[57] Today, a business model that takes advantage of customers to survive is a sign of something broken. With digitization, the customer wins, or the company dies.

Netflix original business model, on the other hand, did not care how long you held onto the DVD. Their policy was simple; once you were ready for a new movie, you would just send them the old one. Now, instead of offering a price of $4.99, $5.99, or even $9.99 for a movie for the night, customers could get unlimited rentals for only $9.99 a month. The shift to abundance for Netflix—and now Amazon Prime and Apple TV—devastated Blockbuster, Redbox, drive-in movie theatres, and the traditional popcorn butter sticky floored movie theaters.

Netflix continued to disrupt itself, further digitizing and offering streaming services directly—first, streaming content from a box connected to your TV set, and then to an app on your Smart TV and mobile devices. These services moved customers from subscription DVDs to streaming, leading to even further dematerialization, demonetization, and democratization of TV and movies. In 2020, Netflix had more than 180 million subscribers worldwide and is on track to generate over $20 billion in revenue.[58] That doesn't even account for how much money the company loses by allowing users to share accounts! This is soon likely to change too.

Netflix created a company culture document, that Facebook's COO, Sheryl Sandberg said, "may well be the most important document ever to come out of Silicon Valley." The document shares a philosophy that thrives on uncertainty, creativity, and trust—a contrast to the hierarchical culture that dominated much of last century's workplace. In summary:

- Creativity is most important-in procedural work, the best is 2x better than the average. In creative/inventive work, the best is 10x.
- Prioritize discovery over job security-many people love our culture and stay a long time. They thrive on excellence and candor and change.... Some people, however, value job security over performance, and don't like our culture.
- Poor employee behavior is caused by misunderstanding-acting "stupid" is actually caused by a failure of communication. It is a profoundly different view of human nature.
- Unlimited vacation-Netflix vacation policy and tracking. There is no policy or tracking.[59]

Beyond creating a unique culture, Netflix content and streaming service has taken abundance to the next level. Now, there is more streaming content on Netflix than a person can watch in their whole lifetime. As if that were not enough, they went even further and started creating content of their own. One of the first Netflix Original projects was House of Cards, the critically acclaimed drama about a politically motivated couple that ascends the rank of public power. The show was an instant hit, and Netflix flexed its muscle, attracting new subscribers with every new piece of unique content.

Netflix has the biggest mouthpiece in the world with its subscription base. Whatever they want to promote is sure to explode in popularity. Other Netflix Originals—like *Making a Murderer*, *Stranger Things*, *Orange Is the New Black*, *Black Mirror*, and *Tiger King*—became monumental pieces of pop culture days after they were first released. Instead of waiting for one episode per week like most cable shows, Netflix purposefully gives you the full season at once. The instant streaming, combined with the release of finished seasons, has created a new phenomenon we didn't know we wanted: binge-watching.

Netflix alone made binging cool. In the days of cable and network TV, nobody would proudly exclaim they watched TV for six hours straight, but in the world of abundance, long binge sessions are necessary to stay relevant in your co-workers' TV discussions at the watercooler or on a Zoom call.

What makes Netflix so brilliant is that their abundance model has no genre, no format, and no censorship. While their TV series and original movies are dominantly powerful, the best example of Netflix's power was their revival of stand-up comedy. For a content devouring audience, Netflix Original stand-up specials answered that hunger: ninety-minute sets from the top comedians in the world.

For a comedian, the ninety minutes of a stand-up set is not ninety minutes of work. It is years and years of tailoring jokes. However, in the abundance model, Netflix doesn't have years to wait. Netflix needs content and it needs it now. Before too long, Netflix ran out of A-list comedians whom they could record. The solution? They manufactured comedians and made a new generation of comics famous.

Relatively unknown comics went from pounding the open-mic circuit and traveling road gigs to becoming overnight superstars with one Netflix special. Comedian diversity took a huge step forward, with women getting the attention and platform they deserved. Comedy legends like Jerry Seinfeld, Dave Chapelle, and Chris Rock even returned from retirement to cash in, signing deals to the tune of $100 million, $60 million, and $40 million respectively. The abundance of content, the abundance of money, and the abundance of viewers.

Nightclub, or Netflix and chill?

The Pixel Party

Kodak is an epic example of what happens on the ugly side of disruption. Kodak was a camera and film photography giant. In the 1990s, they had $19 billion in sales and over 145,000 employees worldwide.[60] Then the film industry became digitized with the advent of the digital camera. In 2012, Kodak filed for bankruptcy.

Here's the unfortunate part of that story: Kodak invented the digital camera.

In the past, Kodak films documented the world. They were king in an industry with very little competition, and they kept innovating. One of the most notable innovations was the digital camera, invented by Kodak employee Steve Sasson in 1975. Digital technology can be deceptive at first, and Kodak was deceived. The resolution was a grainy 100 by 100 pixels (0.01 megapixels), a far cry from today's 12-megapixel iPhone.[61] While Kodak later used digital camera technology in a high-end capacity, they ignored the consumer digital camera altogether, not wanting to disrupt their lucrative film business-a rather small way of thinking. Of course, the technology of the first digital cameras was crude, yet the exponential curve of innovation iterates quickly, and the technology accelerated from crude to superior in less than a couple decades.

The digital camera disrupted everything about how photos and films were done. First, it eliminated the need for film. Second, digital camera technology became massively popular, as each phone soon swallowed the technology of the digital camera and eliminated the need for a separate physical camera. The technology became democratized in every phone on the market. Third, as the world continued to move digitally, photos were shared digitally and were printed less often.

First Flickr and MySpace, then Facebook, Instagram, and Snapchat proved to be the premier way to share photos. With everyone taking and sharing digital photos, for Kodak, it was a really bad time to be in the photo printing business.

When was the last time we printed a roll of film or even a photograph?

Dematerialization: Digital cameras launched, and photos immediately moved to the cloud. The camera itself disappeared into the phone. Now, even digital frames make photos immediately uploaded to Grandma's credenza.

Demonetization: Photos are free to take, store (unlimited), and share (unlimited) through Facebook, Instagram, Messenger, or text. Digital cameras became cheap to make and sell, and eventually were included in every phone.

Democratization: Everyone has a digital camera in their mobile phone, and the capability to share photos digitally.

Flip Video, a standalone pocket-sized video camera, grew quickly, and was acquired by Cisco for $590 million in stock in 2009.[62] It was promptly shut down two years later as every new mobile phone came with the same video technology. Video was democratized overnight too.

The cost of a smartphone has been driven down to twenty-five dollars,[63] fueling Instagram's picture revolution with a new medium for the masses, affordable nearly everywhere in the world. Disruption is relentless, and it can turn on anybody, even the company that invented the technology.

Craig Killed the News

Rewind to 1993 in San Francisco, California. Craig Newmark was a Case Western Reserve computer science graduate working at IBM for nearly 17 years and moved on to work at several contract jobs until introduced to the world wide web by a coworker at Charles Schwab. Craig was fascinated with the internet and he was anxious to build something online. Soon, Craig launched a mailing list that morphed into Craigslist.org.

In 1995, Craigslist became a portal to the dot-com scene that connected buyers and sellers; it was the first exponential online marketplace. Soon thereafter, Craigslist became the largest classified advertisements listing in the world.

Printed newspapers at the time were making money from a variety of revenue sources—user subscriptions, single edition sales, advertising, and paid classifieds. These newspapers generated a powerful cash flow that could fund an expensive team of diligent, uncompromised journalists and investigative reporters. Teams of objective Ivy League writers, well worth their money, were an esteemed group that wrote for an audience of millions of readers. The peak of journalistic influence provided readers with fact-checked, timely, objective investigative reporting. News had never been more reliable and accountable.

Soon, Craigslist found a few areas where people were willing to pay and started to charge a nominal twenty-five dollars for job postings, car postings, and real estate postings only. Craigslist embodied the demonetization of classified advertisements.

The result was a significant blow to newspaper classified revenue because Craigslist demonetized classified postings with only 0–10% of what customers would pay in the paper, a 10x improvement. With Craigslist, customers also did not have to wait three to seven days for the Wednesday or Sunday newspaper to publish to get calls about their ad. Rather, they got calls instantly and sold their items up to 10x faster than they would using print classifieds. These are all signs of a disruptive exponential business model.

As newspaper classifieds became obsolete, newspapers began to feel the hurt of the draining budget and soon laid off journalists. This resulted in newspapers buying more and more syndicated content and news stories. Sensationalists and bloggers began to fill their empty spots as the news shifted from integrity and objectivity to the trivial and extremely opinionated. The more opinionated pieces were, the more interest they attracted in a world of clickbait. News shifted online, and sensationalized news got clicks from social media. Objectivity, for the most part, died.

As shock jock Howard Stern recognized in the 1990's, people that disliked him listened to him more, and he held listeners longer than the radio competition. The audience was sticking around so they could see what he'll say next.

What bleeds leads has always been the formula for hooking people into the nightly news. The negative news cycle was born many years before, yet now was a science for cable news network's Fox and CNN to follow.

Joe Rogan has emerged as the next generation. Rogan stripped Stern from his title as most listened to shock jock when he landed a $290 million-dollar exclusive deal with Spotify. Now, Rogan's audience is 10x greater than Sterns. Rush Limbaugh and others played politics to continue to sensationalize content with obnoxious and divisive commentary. News was forever changed.

Formerly reliable news reporting gave way to a cycle of politically motivated (and sometimes fake) news that contributed to the election of an unlikely president. Even the president, like many citizens, got his news from Twitter and other unreliable resources online littered with trolls and extreme opinions, slowly consuming any objectivity or point of view, no matter what we believe.

Now, Super PACs fund news. Russia funds news. The Facebook algorithm filters news to our worldview eliminating our ability to serendipitously expand our viewpoint, and political advertisements border on fiction and often slander the opposing candidate in previously unimaginable ways. People have blinders on when interacting with the news stream. Often, a set of beliefs feeds us what we already know and believe, eliminating any other opinions or any potential intellectual growth. We see a world polarized by sensationalism.

Leaders recognize the polluted news and often seek to find the intent and source to inform their decisions. Users often share things that support their worldview, whether true or completely fictional. How we see the world, is how the world sees us. A self-fulfilling trap leads society down a path towards more and more extreme opinions, even leading the law-and-order party to lawlessness. When there is an abundance of viewpoints, we must cut through intention to make decisions based on facts.

Journalism was the first industry to be completely disrupted. Journalism as we once knew it-is dead. Bloggers, shock jocks, and TV personalities thrive in the absence of journalists. Sensationalism has changed the narrative and corrupted the core objective oath journalists previously promised. Now, partisan politics takes center stage on the news every night. CNN and Fox News fight for our attention, depending on our political affiliation.

Today, Craig Newmark donates generously to fight scammers, fake news, and consumer privacy, including a $20 million endowment—paid all at once—to City University of New York (CUNY) Graduate School of Journalism, now the Craig Newmark School of Journalism. Newmark has donated more than $40 million to journalism causes since 2015.[64] The donations were possibly a result of guilt from the inadvertent assassination of journalism. Craig didn't kill journalism intentionally, but therein lies the lesson for the big thinking leader: major change and disruption can have drastic unintended consequences. In Craig's case, demonetizing advertisements through online platforms incidentally dismantled the funding source of objective journalism, and the exponential ripple effect still impacts us today, decades later.

Cryptonite

Even money has taken the leap from coins and bills to bits and bytes. In 2008, a peer-to-peer electronic cash system was born as the infamous Satoshi Nakamoto coined a paper with the same name. Bitcoin launched as an open-source killer-app to eliminate the middleman, let users be the bank, while serving the unbanked and underbanked.

The system of mining and distributed ledger allowed the bank anonymity and privacy, while also providing transparency for every user. Since, Bitcoin and now over 7,000 other cryptocurrencies offer a new asset class as secure as the dollars that fold in our pockets or the gold in a bank. Everything is built on supply and demand. The demand has been so large that even though Bitcoin is an early teenager, $1,000 invested 10 years ago is worth hundreds of millions of dollars, making many Bitcoin millionaires and billionaires.

Blockchains have created a system to record owning "digital things." As the internet is an information machine, blockchain is a trust machine. Blockchain creates a decentralized trust mechanism through cryptography, timestamps, and distributed ledgers that others can verify. Blockchain will evolve into a distributed business model, which is open-source, free, and connected to every dual authenticated smart phone in the world. Assets like Ethereum are built on the blockchain with the ability to attach smart contracts to the transaction. Smart contracts automatically execute all or part of the agreement, which is written into the code. This creates trust that whatever the agreement, it will go down as agreed upon. The blockchain will start to become part of nearly every industry, just as the internet before it. The future blockchain will be built on top of the internet as we are already seeing a lack of trust from fake news, data hacks, scams, and fraud appearing everywhere someone is connected.

Blockchain, meanwhile, has its own deceptive history as it evolved over nearly 20 years, prior to Bitcoin. David Chaum founded DigiCash in 1989 in a paper titled "Blind Signatures for Untraceable Payments," started the movement towards a digital currency. Later in 1991, Stuart Haber and W Scott Stornetta described a "cryptographically secured chain of blocks," giving birth to the idea of blockchain. In 1998, Nick Szabo launched Bit-Gold, yet the world was still not ready for this idea. It wasn't until 2008 when the mortgage-backed meltdown nearly brought the financial world to a stop did an opportunity for the first successful cryptocurrency arrive. Satoshi Nakamoto seized the opportunity and Bitcoin was launched successfully with its own sceptics and long period of deceptive growth. Today cryptocurrencies represent over 2.4 trillion-dollar market capitalization, Bitcoin still the largest share of that, yet alt coins are starting to create a very volatile investment for thrill seekers. The key is that this is digitizing another business and investors that have stayed in for long-term have yielded unprecedented results, those in for a quick buck have generally lost or exposed themselves to exceptional risk.

The downside of bitcoin is it uses more energy than some countries and as bitcoin become more widespread, more energy will be needed with the mining and distributed ledger model. By 2024, Bitcoin will use more energy than the entire country of Italy.[65] This is not a sustainable solution for the future and will likely create backlash, prompting us to find a more efficient way to manage the blockchain in the future. Even crypto hype-man Elon Musk announced in May 2021 that Tesla would no longer accept Bitcoin, due to its negative impact on the environment. A bold statement that sent cryptocurrencies in a tailspin. Regardless, this industry is here to stay and pandoras box has been opened, there is no going back.

Further, the United States federal government has now begun exploring a digital dollar and China launched the first national digital currency, the digital yuan. China also can give us a glimpse into a digital world as currency has disappeared with SMS money transfer apps WeChat and Alipay. This asset class has already changed the way we look at money as more and more people funnel money into these assets and the pandemic jumpstarted a movement towards digital money throughout the world, prompting the biggest rise of a new asset class in history.

REFLECTION

What we resist persists. In Pixel Party, Kodak fell to its demise after inventing, and then ignoring, the digital camera. In Death to Blockbuster, Redbox and Blockbuster couldn't pivot to compete with Netflix. Lastly, newspapers and journalism ignored the threat of demonetized ads ultimately leading to its destruction. In Exponential Theory, our biggest threats can be unexpected, yet standing right in front of you.

- What industry force could disrupt your company?
- If your company had to pivot, what would it do?
- How can you digitize your business model?
- How can you use mobile technology in your business model?
- What unintended consequences could your disruption create?
- How can you disrupt yourself like Netflix did when they moved from DVDs to streaming?

Chapter 5.

Becoming a Tech Company

"Every company is now a technology company."
—Gary Shapiro, Consumer Technology Association

The Pizza & Coffee Wars

As disruption through digitization continues to spread, it provides companies with opportunities to capitalize on the digital habits of their customers. The brands that can make the customer experience a digital one wields a major advantage over their competitors, regardless of industry. Domino's Pizza and Starbucks Coffee are two brands that effectively capitalized on changing customer habits, and as a result, are now titans in their respective food and beverage industries.

In 2008, Domino's Pizza stock value hit rock bottom. By 2020, its stock value was 112x higher.[66] It is the only company growing at a faster rate than Facebook, Amazon, Apple, Microsoft, or Google in that same period.[67] It is one of the few businesses able to thrive throughout the global coronavirus pandemic. The exponential growth of its brand was possible thanks to one crucial pivot: Domino's stopped being a pizza company and became a tech company that sells pizza. It all started with an "We're Sorry for Sucking" advertising campaign with the CEO talking directly to the campaign admitting the many flaws and shortcomings from Domino's and the pizza industry as a whole. At the end of the commercial shares a simple promise that Domino's would do better. Only Popeye's Chicken Sandwich war against Chick-fil-a's chicken sandwich empire that launched them into viral relevance in November 2019 created better results for a fast-food company. Yet, Domino's was not focused on a short-term spike, it wanted a long-term strategy. So, it decided to invest in becoming a technology company.

Domino's armed themselves with an aggressive investment in software and digitization of the supply chain, an internal commitment to innovation, and a fresh new menu based on rapid prototyping and customer feedback. Domino's enlisted its 17,000 stores in the Pizza War.[68] The result was a digital platform, a way for the customer and the company to interact with each other digitally, engaging customers via text, emojis, e-mail, apps, and/or websites. Domino's became more relevant to its customers by showing up where customers spent their time.

Domino's has created a digital platform in the form of a mobile app and has integrated everything into one process that provides users with digital services they did not know they needed. A pizza tracker tells customers when their order is in the oven. A push notification is shared when the delivery driver is around the corner. Customers don't even have to yell out to their family when the pizza arrives; there's a mass alert function called the "dinner bell."

As Domino's has adopted the digital platform to work with customers, its business has grown exponentially. This growth can be attributed to the following: First, the app has made the user experience so easy that Domino's is now always part of the consideration set for pizza delivery. Second, the app has provided a direct link to its company in every user's pocket. This has allowed Domino's to dramatically grow its footprint. At dinner time, the app sends push notifications directly to the customer's screen with suggestions for dinner pizza orders with special offers. They have even enabled text and emojis to order pizza. Through digitization, they have won over customers, and the war on pizza. Domino's is an excellent example of the power of thinking big.

Starbucks has also pivoted from a coffee company to a tech company that sells coffee. The Starbucks digital platform, much like Domino's, offers customers a glimpse at potential digitization of a business. For example, the app provides users with the ability to order their beverage online, arrive at a Starbucks, head straight to the beverage rack, and walk out with their order. In essence, this was Starbucks disrupting itself. Starbucks' previous value proposition, otherwise known as a "selling point" for customers, used to be about the atmosphere, customer service, and experience ordering from a barista off a menu laced with words made up by corporate marketing, straight from the coffee houses in Italy. With its platform, Starbucks cut out waiting in line, customer service, and atmosphere altogether and improved customer experiences throughout the ordering process.

Most importantly, though, Starbucks was able to make cash disappear through its app. Allowing all payments to be made through the app—whether ordering ahead or in-store—this saved the customer time. Really, it just made them forget how much money they were spending. It was as if they managed to turn real, hard-earned money into imaginary "Star-bucks." When paying with monopoly money, the customer spends a lot more.

An auto-reload feature to hold an account balance pushes the customer to keep spending. Starbucks customers now keep more money on the app than most banks have in their vaults. Starbucks hoards more than $1.6 billion in pre-purchased value on its app.[69] Starbucks' digital platform has made it the coffee house of choice. Its success has created the most penetrated coffee house in the world with over 32,500 locations, often appearing in multiple locations in highly trafficked areas.[70]

Lastly, both the Domino's and Starbucks apps have been able to gamify the user experience. At Dominos, customers collect "Pieces of the Pie" with each purchase, while at Starbucks, users collect "Stars." The imaginary rewards can be redeemed for free products, which incentivizes customers to purchase more or try new items. The platform, obviously, can connect deeper with a customer than ever before, and the results are a greater brand affiliation, and more importantly, revenue.

While companies like Domino's and Starbucks are pivoting to become tech companies, there are some companies that were already born digital. These companies started on the Apple or Google App Store, and their app could be their entire business. Companies like Uber and Airbnb come to mind.

Apps have created a self-contained marketplace for consumers and producers to meet and conduct business. The Uber marketplace has connected drivers and passengers, and ridesharing occurs. In the Airbnb marketplace, renters and owners meet and rent a property. Thus, these companies' apps are literally building their own marketplaces and adding value by bringing the two parties together, much like how Craigslist brought together buyers and sellers in the early days of the internet.

Building their own marketplaces makes these companies appear seemingly out of thin air. Of course, that means a leaner, more agile company is born, without the burden of massive overhead that competitors bear. The marketplace then disrupts their industry competition at a rapid pace as they race through the 6Ds framework. A marketplace born online in the app store is lean, iterative, agile, scalable, and undoubtedly, exponential.

The Hotel Hitmen

Airbnb disrupted the trillion-dollar travel industry with its new marketplace that set out to connect landlords with couch surfers. Airbnb started with just two guys— co-founders Brian Chesky and Joe Gebbia—and in a matter of a few years, the company has been able to disrupt business for major long-standing brands like Hilton and Marriott. The concept of Airbnb is not a new one: people have been crashing on couches and spare bedrooms for as long as they've been traveling. What is new and successful for Airbnb is the digital marketplace that proved that spare couches and bedrooms were marketable.

Airbnb was able to get off the ground in the first place because of the movement toward a sharing economy. Again, this is a new economy that enables customers to share nearly everything with each other: houses, cars, boats, dresses, etc. The outcome of the sharing economy is twofold—those who own goods in the market make money from them, while those who don't own goods are able to access them for a fraction of the cost. Owners pay off their debt faster from buying the asset, and users don't go into debt. Win-win. This has enabled greater access to property rental without ownership and monetization of ownership.

The sharing economy offers cheaper alternatives to the consumer, a win for current owners or non-owners. If a user can spend $5,000 in a year on ride sharing to get around town, why would they buy a new $60,000 car and worry about all the other expenses? If a traveler can stay in an apartment for three hundred dollars for a vacation, why would they spend $1,200 on a hotel? The potential losers in the sharing economy are the car manufacturers and major hotel brands as new alternatives lower demand.

Hotel brands are built on the assets they own (property, hotels, golf courses, etc.). The hotel business model was built on occupancy and, like Blockbuster, scarcity. Major ownership was simultaneously their biggest competitive advantage and their weakness. Sharing companies, like Airbnb, are the opposite—they own nothing. The end product for the customer, however, is the same: a place to sleep. Because Airbnb doesn't own anything (and has no overhead), it can provide consumers with a significant cost advantage. This would never have been possible had it not been for the digital marketplace to leverage the sharing economy.

In August 2007, the concept for "Air Bed and Breakfast" was born. By April 2009, Airbnb secured Sequoia Venture seed funding. By summer 2011, there were more than two million cumulative nights booked on Airbnb. It moved from conception to millions of stays in just four short years.[71] [72] This is the same amount of time it takes to build a hotel.

The genius in the marketplace is that Airbnb eliminated hoteliers just to become the digital hotelier. Expedia eliminated travel agencies just to become the digital travel agency. Uber eliminated cab dispatches just to become the digital cab dispatch. All these companies rode digital disruption to the top of their industries and became Unicorns, startups worth over $1 billion.

Interestingly, the research found that Airbnb guests stayed, on average, twice as long as hotel guests. They spent more money on their trip, and about 42% of guest budgets were spent in local neighborhoods. Curiously, 80% of guests said they wanted to explore specific neighborhoods.[73] The digital native is starkly different from the non-digital consumer. So, while all Airbnb's don't have standardized spas and swimming pools—and few have daily housekeeping—what they do have is dynamic (rated) listings at a cheaper price per square foot. Large families can now travel again. Couples can do staycations at local Airbnb's. Twenty-somethings can get together at homes that are not theirs for a party. Groups can rent houses for the Super Bowl. The list goes on and on.

Through its marketplace, Airbnb was able to dramatically disrupt hoteliers. The dematerialization was significant. The front desk and concierge were replaced with the app, instructions, and a guest book. The building, like a massive hotel, was replaced with the already existing properties. The staff—cleaning, maintenance, landscaping, bartenders, line cooks, and bellmen—were all removed from the equation. The result was a significant demonetization as few costs enabled lower room prices. At its core, the sharing economy is built on democratization. Still, Airbnb hosts can compete by providing any additional services they think will set them apart and book more nights for their property. Guest books give secrets to the neighborhood and reviews give insight into every experience.

What's important about the Airbnb marketplace was not just the ability to disrupt, but the ability to grow. While using the sharing economy was a way to disrupt the hotel industry, it was also a way to grow faster than hotels. Because Airbnb doesn't own a single property, its cash can be spent on expanding its network through the app rather than on building another hotel. The cost is one thing, but the time is almost more important. To build a hotel offering three hundred new rooms could take years. Airbnb could run an aggressive marketing campaign in a new market and get three hundred new room listings on its site in weeks, days, hours, and now minutes.

As expected, the big thinking company grew exponentially. Airbnb has now become the largest hotel chain without owning a single property. It now has more than seven million listings in 220 countries and counting.[74] Marriott, its closest competitor, owns 1.1 million rooms in 130 countries.[75] By 2020, Airbnb has hosted over 500 million guests, now averaging two million per night and averaging six guests checking in every second. The average revenue to hosts is $185 a night worldwide.[76] The company is valued at more than $35 billion, according to its last capital raise, again without owning anything.[77] In comparison, Marriott is valued at only $28 billion while owning 6900 properties. [78]

Airbnb now rents spare bedrooms, apartments, tiny houses, castles, treehouses, and yachts. It is rapidly expanding across the globe and empowering consumers in new ways. Room listers are making money, and room renters are saving money. Great experiences (plus the savings) make users want to go on more trips or check-in permanently, as digital nomads check out of ownership completely and rent places in exotic locations with local currencies. The economic impact of the new model creates lots of local jobs, in addition to allowing visitors to stay longer and spend more money in local economies wherever they travel. With a digital platform, Airbnb was able to go from its couch-surfing conception to the largest hotel/home rental in the world in thirteen years. The platform yields unprecedented power and is just another success story of thinking big and the exponential theory.

The Taxi Slayer

Uber became the highest-valued startup in the world by building a platform marketplace between car owners and passengers. Much like Airbnb, Uber tapped into the sharing economy and disrupted transportation as we know it. Uber also helped popularize a new economy—the gig economy—while wielding even more disruptive power. Society embraced Uber's marketplace so heavily that Uber continues to grow as it pivots into bikes, delivery, and logistics. Uber even acquired Postmates, a food delivery company, furthering its market share.

Uber is the most disruptive marketplace to date. At face value, the concept is obvious. A consumer needs a ride, calls a ride through the platform (app), and a ride appears in minutes. An algorithm optimized downtime for drivers and schedules the most convenient routes. The marketplace is a disruptive business model. The taxi disappeared into a service on an app in every phone (dematerialized). The cost of rides dramatically decreased (demonetized), and anybody was able to download the app as a driver or passenger, then matched by an algorithm in nearly every market around the world (democratized).

What's really compelling about the Uber equation is that it extends beyond the consumer half, and into the producer half. Like Airbnb, the sharing economy is at play when those who own cars (producers) can share them and make money from them. However, Uber's marketplace went a step further with the gig economy, which was basically mainstream freelancing. Uber became a side hustle for some or a full-time contractor job for others, as car owners drove the cars for Uber themselves. In the gig economy, there's no need for nine-to-five schedules or bosses; you can clock into the marketplace at will and make as much money as you want.

Uber's marketplace disruption and popularity made it essential for life. Uber became a verb like so many other companies before it, including Google and Facebook. Uber knew what was coming next: another disruption. How does one stay the big fish in the small pond? They eat the rest of the fish while they're still small.

Yet Google, Tesla, and Apple have now entered the autonomous car industry, a parallel industry pushing transportation into a new paradigm. The autonomous car will inevitably remove human drivers (dematerialize), demonetization will exponentially lower transportation costs (because humans are the most expensive part of the equation), and democratization will put autonomous features in every car in the future. The idea of owning a car will be absurd as everyone will get around using autonomous cars. Uber's current business model will surely be disrupted by autonomous cars, so it has had to get ahead of the game even if that has meant purposefully disrupting itself, just like Netflix did before them.

What does that mean for Uber? It has already started with UberCopter and is now working on flying cars.[79] Uber understands that it will need to disrupt itself to ride the next wave. It is possible that Uber will become less of a company, and more of a utility—like gas, electricity, or running water. It is likely that transportation will become a subscription. Ridesharing, as it rides the curve of disruption, will eventually become free or nearly free. We can reimagine unlimited transportation for a flat fee each month.

Companies like Mercedes Benz (Daimler) are likely to leverage their brand into autonomous car fleets if they can replace their dealerships with fleet management services. Someday, the general population might ride around in Mercedes Benz autonomous cars for everyday trips. After all, we'd prefer these luxury brands over Ford, Toyota, or Honda for the incremental or non-existent price differential. The luxury brand will be dematerialized (as they will no longer sell cars, they will manage a network or fleet of autonomous cars), demonetized (they will drive cost down to push others out of the market), and democratized (they will give access to quality transportation for everyone), all while finding a better business model, enabling them to make money from the utility and not the marketing and sale of assets. A car will go from creating a one-time profit per sale to creating a profit every month, 10x the value created by each asset. Car manufacturers will have to shift to a new digital model or die.

Potentially, large infrastructure projects like light rail and other forms of public transportation will be a waste of time and resources, as autonomous cars will be significantly more efficient. Also, traffic engineers estimate that autonomous cars could increase traffic volume by 40% in the city and 80% on the highway in a fully autonomous world.[80] Autonomous cars do not collide as they will likely communicate with each other and avoid collisions. This will save 1.35 million lives annually in accidents globally.[81] As risk evaporates, so too will car insurance. Ownership also becomes an option with a full fleet of cars roaming around at your beck and call, further demonetizing, dematerializing, and democratizing transportation in the process. Uber could ultimately win the vehicle wars, pushing into flying cars and driving the cost down to compete with fleets on the streets. Soon, visions of floating cars in *Star Wars* megacities, hoverboards from *Back to the Future*, or George Jetson-style commutes could become a reality.

REFLECTION

How we spend our days is how we spend our lives. Focusing on personal habits and putting in the work will help us reach our goals. Becoming a Tech Company is about change, disruption, and speed.

- What technology could help you reach your goals faster?
- What can you change to become a tech company?
- What alternative industries could disrupt your company?
- What technologies could speed up your company's execution?
- What components of the sharing (Airbnb) or gig (Uber) economies can you use in your business?

Chapter 6.

Finding the Massive Transformative Purpose

"10,000,000,000,000,000,000,000,000,000,000,000,
000,000,000,000,000,000,000,000,000,000,000,000,000,
000,000,000,000,000,000,000"
—Definition of a Google, 10^100

The New Toothbrush

The internet is much simpler than we think.

Most people use the internet to do one of the following: search, browse, check email, and/or use social media (including posting photos or watching videos). Apps used for accessing and sharing information across the internet have been dubbed "killer apps," because of the massive disruption each one has caused.

For any app, being an industry leader is tremendously powerful. Google leads in four of five major areas.

Chrome is the #1 browser[82]

Gmail is the #1 email provider

YouTube (owned by Google) is the #1 video streaming service[83]

YouTube is the #2 most visited website (behind Google)[84]

The only company that beats Google in any category is Facebook, which leads in social media. Google+ (Google's answer to Facebook) failed miserably to find relevancy with users. Google executives even attempted to buy Facebook early on. If successful, Google might own the entire internet experience today. The company's dominance is incredible for a company that is just old enough to drink. Google has found a way into every part of our digital lives, but it was not always so dominant.

Originally, Yahoo ruled the web experience. At its peak in 2000, Yahoo was worth roughly $125 billion.[85] It was the highest valued company in the world at the time. The name, the yodel, and the friendly logo all became synonymous with internet usage.

Yahoo's momentum, market share, and deep pockets should have rendered Yahoo the dominant internet company for the next few decades. Instead, their leadership failed to develop a Massive Transformative Purpose (MTP) to guide the organization. An MTP is a "highly aspirational tagline,"[86] a key component for big thinkers because it makes an organization focus on growth. Without an MTP to guide them, Yahoo was stuck in an innovation deficit and ultimately confused its customers, leading to the company's demise.

How did Google manage to escape the same fate?

Larry Page, the co-founder of Google with Sergey Brin, wanted to create a technology like a toothbrush: something users would use more than once a day, which would make their lives easier.[87] On average, Google processes 5.8 billion search queries a day.[88] Not only did Larry Page create technology that is useful–useful is the new cool.

"We want to build technology that everybody loves using, and that affects everyone. We want to create beautiful, intuitive services and technologies that are so incredibly useful that people use them twice a day. Like they use a toothbrush. There aren't that many things people use twice a day."

—Larry Page

Page's early mindset led to the creation of an MTP that pushed Google to its current level of dominance: "organize the world's information." This MTP is incredibly broad yet provides the bowling bumpers to hit a strike nearly every time. Focusing on organizing the world's information provided Google a clear vision and boundaries for its innovation. Products and services that organize data are at the forefront of Google today—Chrome, Google Drive, Gmail, and the rest of the G Suite. Without the vision and boundaries set forth by its MTP, Google would have likely ended up like Yahoo. Google also did not stray away from its home page experience, barely changing the look since the launch.

Nonetheless, Yahoo couldn't figure out what it was good at or what it should innovate toward. One of its (many) mission statements was to "strive to inspire, delight, and entertain." This lack of clarity helps explain its consistent innovation missteps.

At one time, Yahoo's exponential technology was its new cutting-edge formula to develop pay-for-clicks and monetize the web experience. Yahoo wielded vast revenue power with its novel advertising arm, combined with its large user base. Yahoo seemingly had it all.

In an effort to inspire, delight, and entertain, Yahoo started buying up innovation. Flush with cash, it was making splashy purchases to fulfill its mission. Yahoo bought Broadcast.com from Mark Cuban as the premier pre-YouTube streaming service. Yet timing is everything; the bandwidth didn't support the technology and the world was not ready for streaming video.

YouTube, of course, turned out to be fantastically inspiring, delightful, and inspirational as bandwidth increased. YouTube was able to become all those things because it was not trying to do any of them. YouTube, acquired by Google and sharing its MTP, was organizing all the world's videos, and just so happened to become inspiring, delightful, and inspirational as users rated, shared, and posted videos at an exponential rate.

YouTube is now one of the biggest websites in the world, in part because of its shared MTP with Google. Estimations for YouTube's standalone value vary greatly, with some analysts arguing that the company is worth over $300 billion, making it one of the top twenty most valuable companies in the world.[89] Just to make it sting worse for Yahoo, Google bought YouTube in 2006, while Yahoo bought the now-defunct Broadcast.com in 1999. The timing difference shuttered Yahoo's chance at video dominance. It left Yahoo still shooting in the dark to inspire, delight, and entertain. Yahoo kept acquiring, and purchased GeoCities, Flickr, and Tumblr. Including Broadcast.com, Yahoo spent almost $10 billion on these four acquisitions. [90]

The MTP consciously directed Google to a moment of overarching success and innovation. Yahoo and Google began with similar stories, but over time, their stories had dramatically different endings. Yahoo eventually sold to Verizon for just $5 billion in 2017, just 4% of what it was worth at its peak. Google is one of five trillion-dollar companies in the world, worth 200x more than what Yahoo sold for.[91]

When the World Wide Web was created, essentially the largest database ever was born. Massive connectivity was just beginning, and soon, all human knowledge would go online. There was one major problem, though: the World Wide Web was a lawless, disorganized mess with no standardization and little collaboration.

Larry Page unleashed a new technology, a search algorithm leveraging spiders and the now-famous PageRank algorithm. This algorithm simplified the online search experience to create the most relevant experience for the user who searched with Google. Within a few years, Google monopolized internet search and today still fields over 90% of global search queries.[92] Google makes information accessible to anyone and anywhere nearly instantly.

The sheer volume of searches has made Google a rich company beyond any of its founders' beliefs. At one time, Google's founders were going to sell to Excite for less than $1 million dollars. Yet, Google lucked into revenue streams (like advertisements and paid search results) to capitalize on the ridiculous number of search queries it processed in a day within its search engine. Google is now immensely powerful. Google controls what people see in their search results almost everywhere in the world. When humans have questions, Google has answers. Google became so powerful that it became a verb:

"Just GOOGLE it!"

The PageRank algorithm's advancement of search has vastly improved the world for everyone. Think about how many research papers Google powered by high school students and career academics alike. Flat-out, this book was built on the back of thousands of Google searches. The number of medical, academic, and societal breakthroughs that Google made possible is incalculable. Google has both been the demise of librarians and the death of the Dewey Decimal System. Yet it has freed information for everyone.

Google's algorithms expanded beyond just search and sort and are now predictive in nature. Google continues to push the frontier of artificial intelligence, machine learning, deep learning, and neural networks to find optimal search paths (and advertisements) based on who, what, where, when, why, and how you've used their search engine or other products. Google knows what we might click on next, or what result might be best for us. The accuracy is frightening, and in the near future, Google will know us better than we know ourselves if it doesn't already.

Google's search algorithms built one of the most lucrative businesses in history. There are more than twenty sort algorithms other than PageRank. The Gale-Shapley Algorithm—also known as the stable marriage algorithm, which won a Nobel prize in 1962—created an efficient way to match people through data.[93] This data matching was the basis for the Kidney Exchange Matching Algorithm,[94] which matches organs efficiently and saves lives. Similar algorithms digitized human dating with companies like Match. com, Tinder, Bumble, and more. Algorithms will solve problems as we collect, synthesize, and make data useful to decision making. The power of algorithms is limitless as we layer them with other exponential technologies.

Algorithms powered the Watson computer at IBM to beat the best Chess and Go players in the world. Netflix hosted a $1-million-dollar crowdsourced competition to create an algorithm that continuously improves suggestibility for viewers, leading to a 10% improvement in recommendations of movies and a significantly better experience for users. Machine learning algorithms are leading us toward a time when machines can potentially think like humans, leveraging neural networks and potentially quantum computing. Further, big thinkers and leaders will need to consult machines before they make decisions, as computers can analyze infinite numbers of variables, identifying blind spots and potential human biases passed down by epigenetics.

Ultimately, in the future we will be able to leverage infinite brain power and information to find new ways to solve problems. Humans and machines will work together to better understand the potential outcomes of our decisions. Hopefully, with this power, we will never again tolerate war, environmental harm, or discrimination on race, religion or sexual orientation. Our hope is that even though Google dropped, "Don't be evil," from its Code of Conduct, it continues to apply that consciousness to the code it develops and the employees it hires. [95]

The Power of Data

D ata is the new oil. Data enables AI, machine learning, deep learning, audio assistants, robotics, autonomous cars, drones, and many other exponential technologies to develop and prosper. Exponential technologies create disruption and data is one of the main building blocks behind the current global disruption. Companies have been collecting it for decades, but they didn't know what to do with it.

While Google was organizing the world's information, the company was also getting ridiculously rich in data. When a user searches for something on Google, a multitude of things happen behind the scenes. As Google is racing across the internet to deliver instant search results, it is simultaneously extracting information from each search query: who is searching, what they're searching, when they're searching, where they're searching, why they're searching, and how they're searching.

With this data, Google improves internet searching for everyone. Google can suggest searches for most users before they even type their search into the search bar. Most of these search suggestions are in real-time, adapting to other users' Google searches instantly. Anything hot, relevant, scandalous, dangerous, funny, cute, or impending—Google knows what information the user wants before they do, and that is the power of using data to create proactive results. Google has focused on creating the best user experience (UX) in a simplified way more than any company in history.

Consider the power of data with Google Maps. After acquiring Waze, which crowdsources traffic with thousands of users roaming about every city in the world, Google reads traffic instantly and constantly updates the user's navigation to provide the fastest route. As the data builds up, Google learns trends with machine learning and continually optimizes. Google knows rush-hour traffic better than those who commute in it every day.

Combine the data Google gets from searches, browsing, e-mail, social media, Google mobile phones (Android), and Google Apps on iPhones, and suddenly, Google knows almost everything about everyone, everywhere.

With data as an exponential tool, it's possible to create revenue where previously there was none. The goal used to be to sell a customer a product and then try and get them to buy more. Now, with data, the goal isn't just to sell a product, it is to get customers' data. When data is the currency and the user creates the data, the user becomes the actual product. Google is not selling the data of the user, it is selling ads from the data of the user, and it is a fair deal—Google is a tool for users, and in turn, users are a tool for Google.

Google's abundance of data and the ability to mass-collect it is a fundamental building block of the exponential theory. With data, we can extrapolate almost anything, from information on customers to personal health information, and beyond.

Powered by data, Google was able to launch the safest web browser ever, Google Chrome. Using all its collected data, Google was able to recognize unsafe websites and warn consumers during their browsing. After all, Google needs to keep its product (us) safe if it wants to keep harvesting (our) data for money. As a result,

Google Chrome has nearly two-thirds of the market share of all browsers.[96]

Chrome browser users make the same reasonable sacrifice as Google search users. Chrome makes the internet easy to use, and in exchange, sees everything you do on the internet. The data treasure trove—which used to be simply what users searched—exploded. Google doesn't just know all our search queries; it now knows what we browse. Google didn't stop there: with Gmail, Google Docs, Google Apps, Google Ads displaying on other websites, and Android, Google knows what we said in our emails, who is collaborating on what document, what was said in an elevator to a friend, and everywhere and anywhere we go.

Google is the God of the internet, an all-knowing power that we hope uses its power for good and not evil.

Google's army of engineers get to spend 20% of their time innovating. One of those innovations was a better email platform.[97] Google was able to provide the best email product for free. Making Gmail free was obvious. If the user is the product, Google wants as many users as possible and can pay for it with advertisements inside the product and search. Yahoo, AOL (America Online), and Hotmail (owned by Microsoft) could not compete; all these email providers slowly lost the war on email. The masses shifted from these old email paradigms to a better experience with Gmail. Having a Yahoo, AOL, or Hotmail account is a symbol of a previous era.

Just like how Google remained clean and crisp with its search engine design, it did the same with email. Gmail is the easiest email to use on the market, and it's even easier for users to get a Gmail account. With all its data, Google has the best spam filters, the best predictive typing, and the best email address recognition software. These are just a handful of the selling points for Gmail.

As Google went on to create more products for the user, it seamlessly integrated user experiences between apps. Google Docs came out as a great way to collaborate with people and counter Microsoft Word, Excel and PowerPoint dominance, particularly if those people also use Gmail. Google built out the rest of the G Suite in the same way—it became significantly easier for users to stay in the Google stratosphere, so most people didn't deviate from it. Adding in Chromebooks and good bandwidth, Google created very low-cost Android tablets and laptops that have begun to change the way we compute, moving nearly everything to the cloud. This drove down the cost of a tablet or laptop to something that nearly everyone in the world could buy with a month's salary. Google democratized access.

Google's command over these killer apps has made it the starting point for most people on the Internet. However, when the world went mobile, Google needed to follow suit. Google made another genius move to acquire Android in 2005, leading it to be the number one brand in smartphones in the world. According to IDC Research, Google now powers seven out of eight smartphones in the world with the Google Android operating system.[98] Apple's iPhone often gets the hype, yet Android has become the dominant system by focusing on the software and letting others deal with the hardware. Much like how Microsoft became dominant as the software inside the computer, Google is the software inside most phones.

We're the Product

Only when we consider our privacy do we realize how much Google knows. Maps, Android smartphones, and Chrome internet logins track a user's physical location.

Google knows where we are. Search queries are more obvious since the user plugs that information directly into Google. Google knows all our questions, our fears, and our late-night thoughts. Google knows everything in Gmail, so it knows what we say about our co-workers, the best times to check our inbox, the videos we watch, and which emails we ACTUALLY read. Google Home listens to everything in the house; we continue to invite strangers into our homes and yet complain about privacy. Google now knows everything online and offline.

When we're the product, we have no privacy, yet consumers willingly exchange this for the right to use all their products and services for free. However, since some public pushback (or maybe just to set the trend in the digital age moving forward), Google has made some concessions to delete information for users' accounts every eighteen to thirty-six months by default.[99] While this is reassuring to some, it likely won't change much. After all, in the world of accelerating change, eighteen to thirty-six months can be the equivalent of decades of progress.

Eating Alphabet Soup

The Exponential Theory calls for us to learn to leverage data like Google, too. With all the data that Google has accumulated, it's one of the smartest companies in the world. This is how big thinkers at Google took the smartest company in the world and made it the smartest workplace in the world. Just as Google shaped its products, it used data to make its employees productive. Productivity translates into speed, and speed translates into a competitive advantage. Fun workplaces were created, sure, but Google also used data to inform snack placement in every kitchen on its campus. When Google put the healthy snacks on the middle shelf, the sodas on the bottom, and the sugary snacks up high, its staff started to eat better, which created better performance, because there were fewer sugar highs and lows. [100]

Project Aristotle—a tribute to Aristotle's quote, "The whole is greater than the sum of its parts"—examined what makes an effective team at Google. Google examined 180+ teams to find out what makes them work. The team is where productivity happens, ideas are created and tested, and where most (if not all) of the work gets done at Google. So, Google sought out to test productivity in a team. Over two years, Google conducted more than two hundred interviews that looked at 250 attributes, in the hopes of better understanding individual contribution versus team output. Would a superstar on a team have the biggest output?

The answer is no.

Google found out that how team members interact and structure their work was more important than who was on the team. From Project Aristotle, Google learned that there are five key dynamics that set successful teams apart from other teams at Google:[101]

1. Psychological safety: Can we take risks on this team without feeling insecure or embarrassed?
2. Dependability: Can we count on each other to do high-quality work on time?
3. Structure and clarity: Are goals, roles, and execution plans on our team clear?
4. Meaning of work: Are we working on something that is personally important for each of us?
5. Impact of work: Do we fundamentally believe that the work we're doing matters?

Google set out to create teams with these dynamics rather than putting individual talent first. Google's culture can be best described as team-oriented, yet this is another example of Google using data to outperform the rest of Silicon Valley's speed. Google continues to drive change to keep itself in control of the internet, ranking first in the browser, search, email, and video categories.

At the same time, Google continues to expand its footprint. Google knows that reliance on internal innovation alone is a death sentence. Google Ventures scours the world to find and purchase the most potentially disruptive companies it can. So far, Google has acquired more than 230 companies. Companies like Nest make the smart home a reality for Google. With Fitbit, Google enters the personal health market. Google continues to lead innovation in nearly every area it invests in, outgrowing its original 1998 Massive Transformative Purpose (MTP).

In 2015, Google needed to create a new MTP that allowed its other interests to grow independently outside of its core. Unlike Yahoo and other companies that got too big for their own good, exponential leaders Page and Brin took a step back. Eventually, all the exciting ventures and the newly expanded footprint were going to lead Google astray. Thus, Page and Brin created the parent company "Alphabet." Page and Brin continued as co-founders, employees, board members, and controlling shareholders of the trillion-dollar Alphabet, Inc.

On their website, Alphabet frames the future it is excited about with:[102]

- Getting more ambitious things done
- Taking the long-term view
- Empowering great entrepreneurs and companies to flourish

- Investing at the scale of the opportunities and resources we see
- Improving the transparency and oversight of what we're doing
- Making Google even better through greater focus
- And hopefully . . . as a result of all this, improving the lives of as many people as we can

Alphabet has become a collection of companies, and "G" is for Google, nothing else is related to organizing the world's information. Everything from curing cancer with bracelets, automating everything, Wi-Fi everywhere, robotics, and working on many other solutions to "billion person problems." As Larry Page has shared, a problem wasn't considered worthy unless it could solve a problem for a billion people. So, Alphabet has aligned its strategy as a holding company that owns and invests in other companies that can solve billion person problems. This is exponential theory inside a company. This is a company that for the foreseeable future will be involved in some of the most important innovations and launch many more exponential companies.

Google has created the framework for much of Silicon Valley's success, and many former executives and employees have moved on to create hundreds of successful startups outside of Google. Early hires at Google became multi-millionaires and billionaires and moved on to drive growth throughout the Silicon Valley startup ecosystem as founders, investors, and venture capitalists. The multiple generations of success fuel the desire to work at Google. Google has held the title for being one of the best places to work over the last twenty years. Google receives more than two million job applications per year for fewer than six thousand open spots, which means that statistically it is much more difficult to get into Google than into Harvard or Oxford Universities.[103]

Massive Transformative Purpose is a vital tool for thinking big. Nobody does that better than Google, and now Alphabet. Google showed that we must focus on changes that make an impact on over one billion people, which will undoubtedly set them apart from other companies. With accelerating change, and exponential technologies like algorithms and data, the future is bright for Alphabet and its subsidiaries. Unlike Yahoo, which lost its focus, Alphabet has provided us with a roadmap for what to do in case we outgrow our own MTPs.

REFLECTION

The goal is not the end. The journey is the reward. In Exponential Theory, you need to set a massively transformative purpose (MTP) that will allows your organization to grow, retain talent, and withstand a competitive assault or industry shift. The MTP must be incredibly big so that your organization can grow beyond your industry.

- What is your company's MTP?
- Data is the new oil. How can you use data more to assist you grow your purpose?
- How do you define your company culture?
- PageRank algorithm put Google on the map, is there a part of your business model that can be made more efficient with an algorithm?
- What business model could help you scale your business faster?

Chapter 7

Launching Disruption

"Here's to the crazy ones. The misfits. The rebels.
The troublemakers. The round pegs in the square holes.
The ones who see things differently . . . While some may see
them as the crazy ones, we see genius. Because the people
who are crazy enough to think they can change the world,
are the ones who do."
—Rob Siltanen

Timing is Everything

No other event in the brief history of the exponential world was as perfectly timed as Apple's iPhone release in 2007. This moment was so important that we argue that technology will be defined as pre-iPhone and post-iPhone. The iPhone was a major catalyst for mass digitization and mobilization of technology. This was not just another product launch; rather, Apple launched disruption that would forever change the world.

It was a similar moment to when Gates released Windows. The world went digital. Suddenly, people wanted a computer even if they did not think they needed one before. When the iPhone launched, people already had smartphones or flip phones with many of the features. Yet the iPhone made them desire smartphones. Consequently, the world went mobile. In 2007, when Steve Jobs and Apple released the iPhone, they nailed the timing. The guy who created the first iPhone, Marc Porat, did not. He had single handedly laid the vision for the iPhone seventeen years earlier. He was the exponential leader that never was.

The Pocket Crystal

In 1976, Marc Porat was a student at Stanford and had just finished writing his PhD thesis, arguing that the "Information Economy" would be the future of the United States. Information technology, Porat claimed, ". . . would become the dominant driver of the U.S. workforce."[104] Simply put, information technology is "The study or use of systems (especially computers and telecommunications) for storing, retrieving, and sending information."[105] Porat argued that computers would become so powerful that they would build their own economy. This economy would be superior to all previous economies and would fundamentally change how business would be done in the future. Porat defined the future in a way that few had done at this point in history. Porat laid the foundation for exponential theory.

Marc Porat is credited as the first person to coin "Information Economy," the term that encompassed an entire economy built on the use of information technology and the "knowledge workers" that built it.[106] Surely Porat had no idea how important his assertion would become in 1976. Forty-three years later in 2019, *Harvard Business Review* argued that data economy power "could determine the next world order, much like the role that oil production has played in creating economic power players in the preceding century."[107]

Marc Porat was spot on.

Fast forward to 1990. Marc Porat worked on the team that developed the original Macintosh computer at Apple. After the first Macintosh launched, Porat put his heart and soul into a book titled *Pocket Crystal*, explaining a digital and mobile future. Ultimately, Porat left to become co-founder of a company called General Magic, in which Apple owned a minority stake.

The leading vision Porat used to bring partners aboard General Magic with him was also codenamed "Pocket Crystal." This story is wonderfully told in a gripping documentary, *General Magic*, which debuted at the Tribeca Film Festival in 2018. The device, Porat explained to eventual co-founders Andy Hertzfeld and Bill Atkinson, would be able to communicate globally. Instead of residing on a desk, it would fit in the user's pocket. Megan Smith, General Magic team member and former Chief Technology Officer of the United States stated, "Marc came up with this idea that he called a Personal Intelligent Communicator—a smartphone, basically. The whole idea was there."[108]

General Magic, shrouded in secrecy, courted leaders of Apple, Motorola, Sony, and AT&T to sit on General Magic's board and help develop the company, the Pocket Crystal, and the future. In talking to his team about the Pocket Crystal, Porat declared, "You'd wear it all the time, and if there was a fire in your house you'd think, family goes first, and then I grab my Pocket Crystal."[109]

The team went to work developing this unique product. Along the way, they created the modern-day USB connection, Tele-script (the ability for computers to communicate regardless of manufacturers), touch screens, and emoticons.[110] Emoticons, the team explained, were a bunch of cute little animated images that Pocket Crystal users could send to each other. They created smiley faces, hearts, and little animated dudes running away from animated boulders.

Marc Porat was talking about the modern-day iPhone in 1990. His General Magic team was so far ahead of their time—they even created emojis, now a widely used language of texters. Years and millions of dollars were spent on the Pocket Crystal, which ultimately launched and failed. General Magic and Marc Porat were out of the spotlight. Seventeen years later, the future that the team only dreamed about actualized. However, when we're thinking big with the exponential theory, having the idea is only a small part of the success—timing is everything.

The Book of Jobs

In 1983, Steve Jobs and Apple lured marketing guru John Sculley away from PepsiCo to help them take over the personal computer market. Steve Jobs successfully sealed the deal after he made his legendary pitch to Sculley: "Do you want to sell sugared water for the rest of your life? Or do you want to come with me and change the world?"[111]

John Sculley dropped the Pepsi bottle and was soon working at Apple, which was preparing for the first major Macintosh launch. The crown jewel of the marketing campaign came during a commercial in the 1984 Super Bowl. At that time, during the rehearsal of the Macintosh introductions, Steve Jobs told Sculley, "I think of you just like [Steve Wozniak] Woz and [Mike] Markkula. You're like one of the founders of the company. They founded the company, but you [John Sculley] and I are founding the future."[112]

The Apple commercial was a scene from the movie 1984—based on George Orwell's novel *1984*—about a police state that ruled the world with computers. As all the mindless members of the state sat in front of a large screen getting brainwashed by their supreme leader, a blond woman in red and white (symbolizing change and disruption) came running through, crashing a sledgehammer into the screen. There was an explosion, and the commercial's narrator claimed: "On January 24th, Apple will introduce Macintosh. And you'll see why 1984 won't be like 1984."[113]

The 1984 Super Bowl commercial became a cultural icon, and Apple firmly planted itself as the brand that would liberate the masses through their products. The brand was not another Microsoft Office product that littered the office. It was a brand you wanted in your home. A status symbol. Even a tattoo or more likely a bumper sticker sharing users' allegiance to the brand.

However, Sculley was too big for Steve Jobs to wrangle. While Sculley reigned as Apple's chief from 1983 to 1993, sales grew from $800 million to $8 billion.[114] Early on, Jobs was locked in a power struggle with Sculley. Jobs would hold meetings past midnight, send lengthy faxes to teams, and then call follow up meetings at seven o'clock in the morning. The board instructed Sculley to "contain" Jobs, and when he failed, the board removed Jobs' managerial duties in 1993. Jobs resigned to create NeXT, Inc. that same year.

Jobs would return home to Apple after launching NeXT and acquiring Pixar from Lucasfilm's in 1986. For eight years, Jobs built the NeXT operating system and returned to make it the future OS X for Apple. Apple had grown up in Jobs' absence, but many of Apple's early team members shared that the company seemed to lose its soul in the process. Jobs brought the soul back and started to build one of the most beloved brands on the planet.

Steve Jobs, of course, would lead Apple to the top of the world. What made him such an impactful disruptor? He couldn't code. It was debatable whether he could even manage or lead people since according to most accounts he was notoriously disliked by his employees. However, he still had great foresight into what technology could do for society, and how to sell it. Jobs was almost an alien that had a knack for seeing the future.

> "Creativity is just connecting things. When you ask creative people how they did something, they feel a little guilty because they didn't really do it, they just saw something. It seemed obvious to them after a while. That's because they were able to connect experiences they've had and synthesize new things. And the reason they were able to do that was that they've had more experiences, or they have thought more about their experiences than other people. Unfortunately, that's too rare a commodity. A lot of people in our industry haven't had very diverse experiences. So, they don't have enough dots to connect, and they end up with very linear solutions without a broad perspective on the problem. The broader one's understanding of the human experience, the better design we will have."
>
> **–Steve Jobs**

As we have discovered, the vision for the iPhone was not a new one to Apple. However, that's where Jobs' brilliance lies—in the planned and deliberate timing of the iPhone moment's disruption. The iPhone moment was carefully crafted and planned by Jobs' ability to recognize the market. Apple publicly denied the manufacturing of an iPhone or phone product for years, waiting for a time when society would be willing to accept and desire it. Jobs continually fought the launch of the iPhone, thinking they would be relegated to the "pocket protector" crowd. Then, the market aligned, and it was time to launch. A time when consumers wanted a phone, music device, camera, and organizer in their pocket. If they had rushed the iPhone, they could have ended up with yet another failed Pocket Crystal, Newton, or PalmPilot.

The iPhone is the biggest blockbuster of all time and has paved the way for success for many products to come. In 1994, when General Magic's Pocket Crystal launched, there were fourteen million internet users, and one cellphone per one hundred people on Earth, and the first SMS text had been sent just two years prior. Marc Porat and the Pocket Crystal had failed. The world was not ready for it.

So how did Apple know that the world would be ready for the iPhone in 2007?

Let's paint the picture (hindsight, after all, is twenty-twenty). It all started with Newton, Apple's own personal digital assistant, which was launched in 1993 and improved throughout the 1990s, yet ultimately canceled and subsequently widely regarded as a flop. Newton was a slap in the face to General Magic and Marc Porat's efforts, yet all these devices were too early for them to recognize commercial success. In 1997 came the PalmPilot, a competitor and better version of Apple's Newton. Schedules, phone numbers, and more at the touch of a stylus on an efficient touch screen.

For just $399, consumers could buy the PalmPilot Professional with a whopping one megabyte (MB) of storage. The PalmPilot was a fancy upper-class work status symbol. What the PalmPilot did prove was that consumers were moving toward smaller digital products. Consumers were interested in a portable assistant device like the PalmPilot.

At the same time, Steve Jobs—now known as one of the greatest digital disruptors on a mass scale—set out to take over the music industry. Before the iPod, music was sold in stores in the mall or through a mail service called Columbia House, selling eight cassette tapes and CDs for a penny and then hooking users into a monthly subscription service through the mail. Columbia House was the early prototype for Netflix. Sony released the first personal music listening device, the portable Walkman, in 1977. The Walkman played cassettes, and the public was buying into the idea of playing music on the go. But again, Jobs was here for the whole industry, not just a sliver of the market. Another CD or cassette player was not enough to feed Jobs desire for both technological and societal advancement. The new device needed to digitize even CDs and cassettes.

Digital music has demonetized, dematerialized, and democratized the music industry in several waves. Digital music was in development as early as the 1980s, when scientists were researching how to effectively code the same sounds that humans hear. The technology progressed, and the result was the MP3 audio file format that reached prevalence in the 1990s. This file could play songs and albums on computers, and there was soon the ability to convert CDs and other released recordings into an MP3 file format. Most notoriously, Napster was the first peer-to-peer file-sharing network of the MP3, before they were sued by just about everybody for copyright infringement and music piracy.

First, CDs disrupted records, 8-tracks, and tape cassettes when they were able to play music digitally. Then, MP3 players trumped CDs by taking out the need for numerous physical discs. Finally, streaming services like Spotify and Apple Music rendered MP3 players obsolete, as music could now be played on any device connected to the internet.

Apple's answer to Napster was iTunes.

Initially, iTunes was software for Macintosh to manage MP3 files. Only months later, in 2001, did Apple release its own portable MP3 solution: the iPod. Music was well on its way to digitization.

Remember, one of the crucial goals of this new personal tech advancement was that it would do what it promised. The iPod was brilliantly simple with a simple dial: your music, on your time, all the time. The storage on an original iPod was 120 GB, or in marketing terms, one thousand songs. Soon, iTunes became support software for the iPod. The software could help users encode and download their own personal music collection into the MP3 format, and put it right on their iPod. When music went digital, it profoundly changed how many people thought about portable technology. Who wouldn't want to have all their music all the time? Apple fulfilled its goal with the iPod, as they got people to desire it, becoming a huge hit with consumers.

The massive disruption did not really take hold until the iTunes Store was launched in 2003. The iTunes Store was Apple's legal digital music marketplace. Their catalog was dense, and users could purchase whole albums or buy songs individually for just $0.99. This became very disruptive for album sales. This is when iTunes changed everything for the music industry.

Again, with digital disruption, we know three things are inevitable: demonetization, dematerialization, and democratization.

The dematerialization was obvious, as the previous competitor required Compact Discs (CD) or cassettes, and one-thousand-songs-worth of CDs was something that belonged in shelving beneath a stereo, not in the user's pocket.

The demonetization soon followed. The overhead for CDs and cassette tapes was removed through the MP3. So, prices—and music revenue—dropped. In 2002, one year before the iTunes Store, CDs made up 95% of the music industry's revenue and the music industry's revenue was $21.5 billion. Since then, the CD has fallen to a rock bottom low of $600 million out of a total of $11.1 billion (5.5%).[115] iTunes took the money right out of the equation, which quickly took a toll on album sales as singles became the new music purchase of choice.

However, MP3 players like the iPod and its competitors were only the first wave of digital music. Nearly a decade later, music got digitally disrupted again when MP3s were replaced by streaming music services. Music streaming was the truest sign of demonetization; instead of buying an album for $9.99 on the iTunes Store, a streamer could pay for a month of unlimited streaming of any song in the world for $9.99. This adjustment to abundance is no surprise, and the fact that music became nearly free is a symptom of a hyper-competitive global system. Through this massive price drop—and through the collection of unlimited music companies like Spotify, Pandora, and Apple Music—music was finally available to the masses and has been completely democratized. Amazon and Google have now entered the subscription music space, too, and many other industries are now experimenting with their own subscriptions.

iPhone Moment

Fast forward to 2007. Six years have passed since the iPod was first released, and four years since the iTunes Store disrupted the entire music industry. While technology is advancing, consumers themselves are socially changing, too. Small, portable, devices like the iPod are a monstrous success. The world is now a step closer to mobile digitization.

Smartphones have since been introduced to the business world. BlackBerry is the dominant smartphone for corporate types. Yet, while the population is moving toward accepting smartphones and technological advancements, BlackBerry isn't doing the trick for mass consumers.

The BlackBerry, much like the PalmPilot, was nothing more than just a work tool—a faster way to send emails. Both the Black-Berry and the PalmPilot were not quite there with the technology for consumers. As Jobs envisioned, the iPhone was not just a tool, but an extension of the consumer. People needed the iPhone. The media continually asked Jobs if he was going to launch a phone, which he denied all the way until the launch of the iPhone, a nod to his brilliant timing.

In 2005, Nokia had the most popular phones sold worldwide and sold its billionth phone.[116] All had black and white screens, SMS texting with only nine keys, and flip screens. In 2006, consumers started to become disinterested in the flip phone, and Nokia sales started to slip. At the same time, BlackBerry started moving into the consumer market, as people demanded access to email and a browser for the first time on their phones.

Then came the iPhone moment—the most important product launch in the history of mankind. It disrupted hundreds of electronic items as they were dematerialized, demonetized, and democratized into apps on the iPhone.

In June 2007, the iPhone was released to critical acclaim and long lines wrapping around each Apple store. The rest is history.

The iPhone's impact cannot be understated. Not only is it the bestselling gadget ever created, but it is also the most influential. The iPhone has now replaced the need for a camera, GPS device, communication tool, trip planner, and so much more.

"The iPhone is a deeply, almost incomprehensibly, collective achievement," Brian Merchant declares in his new biography of the iPhone, *The One Device: The Secret History of the iPhone.* "Thomas Edison did not invent the lightbulb, but his research team found the filament that produced the beautiful, long-lasting glow necessary to turn it into a hit product," Merchant continues. "Likewise, Steve Jobs did not invent the smartphone, though his team did make it universally desirable. Yet the lone-inventor concept lives on." [117]

As the iPhone launched, Apple soon created an App Store, and the ability to download new apps onto the iPhone creates endless possibilities. The ensuing innovation enabled many of the Unicorn business models that followed. The apps that have most successfully leveraged the infrastructure of the iPhone are Facebook, Twitter, Instagram, Snapchat, TikTok, Spotify, Amazon, LinkedIn, Slack, Uber, Airbnb, Starbucks, Dominos, and Gmail. Mobile games such as Farmville, Pokémon Go, Flappy Bird, and Candy Crush created a new industry altogether, as video games have eclipsed the movie industry in receipts.

The iPhone has also become a data-producing machine. The iPhone has fourteen sensors continuously collecting data on human location, activity, search, and more that companies can leverage. It begs the question, what secrets can you keep from your iPhone or Siri, the first virtual voice assistant?

It's difficult to speculate on the next features of the iPhone, yet if we project a list, we could see future iPhones with high-powered speakers (rivaling much larger speakers today), the ability to project video and conference calls onto any surface, holographs, lidar (lasers) that enhance augmented reality, and enhanced virtual reality capabilities. From there, the iPhone will likely disappear and become wearable: like the Apple Watch, Google Glasses, and layered contact lenses, and thereafter, potentially a bio-implant. The iPhone could become an implant that is enabled first by voice, and thereafter, by thought. Technology is continuing to shrink and disappear.

Beyond the iPhone

Jobs would do it again with the iPad in 2010. Apple could have released the third-generation iPad technology when it released the original iPad, but Apple limited and narrowed the original scope so that it could get to market at the right price. This also allowed Apple a technological advantage for when it inevitably released the third-generation iPad. The iPhone technology was built into a bigger screen and soon took over the tablet market, becoming one of the fastest-growing sales engines for the Apple company. Apple is now focused on using the iPad to replace the laptop as it continues to advance the technology of a laptop into a tablet.

The Apple Watch sells more watches then the entire Swiss watch industry.[118] Apple acquired Beats by Dre, which held a dominant share in the headphone market. The AirPods are now a roughly $8 billion dollar division, which as a stand-alone company would rank as number 384 on the Fortune 500.[119] Apple's global sales for AirPods alone are greater than the entire GDP of some countries.

Learning foresight and timing from Porat, Jobs, and Apple will be important for big thinkers and leveraging the exponential theory. While Apple is likely already thinking well beyond anything we are writing about here, it is still waiting for society to catch up before its next release. This unprecedented understanding of accelerating change and its impact on humans is what sets Apple apart as one of the five biggest companies in the world. We don't know what it is working on, but we do know that whatever it is will be released right on time.

REFLECTION

Attitude is everything. Once Steve Jobs returned to Apple, he was determined to launch disruption and saw how he could change the world.

- Timing is everything, is the timing right for your product or service?

- Like the Super Bowl commercial of 1984-Apple was able to create major hype for their product before it ever hit the market. What ways could you present your idea/product/service as earth shattering as Apple does, without even releasing it?

- Apple Demonetized, Dematerialized, and Democratized the music industry by making music digital with the iPod and the iTunes store. How could you disrupt your business by democratizing part of your business?

- What technologies in your industry have been overlooked and how could they help your company?

Chapter 8.

Leveraging the Viral Loop

"If you are on social media, and you are not learning,
not laughing, not being inspired, or not networking,
then you are using it wrong."
—**Germany Kent, Broadcast Journalist**

Black Lives Matter

O n Tuesday, June 2, 2020, Instagram was full of black screens.

#blackouttuesday

The murder of an unarmed Black man, George Floyd, by Minneapolis police, sparked outrage across the United States and beyond. The amount of time Floyd was illegally restrained—9:24—was captured on social media and sparked a civil rights movement like no other before in history. Millions of people have protested—the world had just endured months of government stay-at-home orders due to the coronavirus pandemic—people flooded city streets across the globe in protest of police brutality. Additionally, millions of users flooded Instagram with black tiles, signaling their solidarity with the Black Lives Matter movement.

Just as the platform was filled with black, many started to question the effectiveness of the campaign. Don't use #BlackLives-Matter because it's burying posts with information! Use #black-outtuesday instead! Then, #blackouttuesday is silencing us, don't use any hashtags at all!

While the mass media ran with the sensational videos of the looting and riots, Instagram told a different story. Millions of users posted videos of peaceful protests, or even more shockingly, instances of police brutality during the protests, all of which directly conflicted with what was on network TV. The last remaining place to find reliable information about protests was quite literally Instagram, with videos by the people, for the people. There were more cameras feeding directly to Instagram than there were body cameras on the police, surveillance cameras on the streets, or news cameras from the sky. It was crowdsourced news that, frankly, was doing a much better job than the media.

This is the impact that digitization has on our population. Social unrest and giving a voice to the unheard is now more efficient than ever. Prior to these protests, other uprisings like the Arab Spring, Occupy Wall Street, Wiki Leaks, Panama Papers, and Cambridge Analytica were made possible by social media movements, some progressive, some devastating. Social networks proved that they're more powerful than both the government and the media combined. Facebook's power to communicate has created fear in both government and media and it's being attacked every day. The most connected generation ever—with mass access and the democratization of digital technology—is changing the world while going "live." Spread across all fifty states and many countries around the world, the George Floyd protests attracted more participants than any civil rights movement in world history. This is the power of tapping into the viral loop. This is the power of thinking big. This is the power of the exponential theory.

#BlackLivesMatter

The Social Network Wars

The stories of Facebook's beginning are etched into pop culture lore. A drunk undergrad, Mark Zuckerberg, created a crude hot-or-not game comparing Harvard coeds (dubbed FaceMash) that crashed the Harvard internet network with its popularity in a few hours. He then (allegedly) stole the idea for Facebook from fellow classmates and rowing Olympians, the Winklevoss twins, who sued Zuckerberg and won. That only added to his legend, complete with his infamous drunk coding binges and all-night parties after he dropped out of Harvard and moved to Palo Alto. He wore flip flops and hoodies to U.S. depositions. There is a lot of myth in the creation of Facebook, but one thing is certain: Facebook has won the social network wars, for now.

Facebook launched in 2004, limited only to Harvard students with verified Harvard email addresses. The site launched as a way to communicate to classmates in lieu of the digital Harvard yearbook, which only allowed users to identify classmates with their school ID pictures. It quickly expanded to Stanford, Columbia, and Yale. Soon thereafter, Facebook opened to all other colleges in the Boston area, the Ivy League, and gradually all universities in the United States and Canada. Facebook was not the first social network, but it quickly became the most popular. The scarcity and limited launch model were only part of the early success in getting people to move from MySpace to Facebook. The idea was that only prestigious peers from prestigious universities would be invited. Essentially, Facebook was selective with its users at first, exclusive over inclusive.

The scarcity model built up demand, yet as the network opened to a new campus, the viral loop showcased an excellent example of the network effect. For example, once someone joined from a new college, they invited all their classmates, and soon everyone was online from that network or university. Nearly everyone joined as the viral loop gained speed and new networks opened. Facebook spread like playing six degrees of separation from Kevin Bacon or tracing patient zero in a virus outbreak. Metcalfe's Law of network power tells us that once the network adds a user, the network's power doubles. There was deliberate and immediate exponential growth once Facebook landed at a university, consumed its population, and then jumped to the next university, the next high school, and the next workplace. Finally, the general public was curious and wanted in.

The other key to the early success of Facebook was relevance, which was overlooked by Google+ and other social networks before it. While relevance was a value proposition for Facebook, it was likely just a happy byproduct of the exclusive roll-out strategy. The community of college students, within their own version of Facebook (based on their network), created relevant content for the user as soon as they joined the network. It was like a huge party on the internet, but the only other people invited were the people you knew or would want to know.

This relevancy ultimately made other networks like Friendster and MySpace irrelevant. Tom Anderson, the founder of MySpace, was the first friend of everyone on MySpace, and it was up to the members to build their network randomly. While MySpace was open to anybody, Anderson was the only friend everyone had in common on MySpace. It was an unorganized party with no filters, a few friends, a lot of spam, and a bunch of strangers.

Facebook, alternatively, recommended that people connect based on schools, friends, content, interests, hobbies, or companies. It also required a verifiable e-mail. This led to a tightly woven viral loop engaging nearly everyone in a network to join. If everybody you know and care about is at the party, you're gonna miss out! This fear of missing out (FOMO) also brings people back to Facebook after they attempt to leave, as emails continue to alert you to the latest meme, picture, video, or post.

In 2005, Zuckerberg launched the high school version and opened to twenty-one universities in the United Kingdom and other universities around the world. Then it expanded eligibility to several companies like Microsoft and Apple, always verifying real people with real email addresses. By the end of 2005, Facebook had six million users, and had reached more than two thousand colleges and over twenty-five thousand high schools throughout the world. Facebook had reached a tipping point. By September 2006, Facebook opened to the world by allowing anyone older than thirteen with a valid email to access it. From there, it has continued to grow to over 2.6 billion people in nearly every country in the world today. [120]

The Viral Loop

A viral loop is a self-sustained mechanism that drives continuous referrals for continuous growth. Facebook's viral loop was so powerful that it was nearly impossible to not get sucked in. As the user and content base grew exponentially, it was easier to cave to the gravitational pull of relative content than it was to hold out. Laggards, grandparents, and technology luddites ultimately became Facebook members because their communities practically forced them to do so. FOMO! The fear of missing out.

When properly executed, the viral loop drives existing customers/users to refer new users, and in turn, gets those newly referred customers to recruit even more users through invitations and sharing relevant content. The cycle is self-sustained, as the process repeats itself. This creates a lasting loop that inevitably leads to exponential growth. As new users are added to the network, they contribute content, and thus the content grows along with the user growth. All the modern social networks we use rely on the viral loop to prop up their business model. After all, what good is a tweet, snap, or video if there's no one to share it with on Twitter, Snapchat, or TikTok?

The viral coefficient is a mathematical way to determine the effectiveness of the viral loop. Specifically, it calculates how many new users are added by existing users on the platform. Facebook's viral coefficient is greater than any other company in history, and it connected the world by leveraging pre-existing offline networks, like work and school. Everyone continued to invite all members of their networks to Facebook, increasing the viral coefficient. Soon all our different networks had a community to communicate and all of our feeds united in one place.

The viral loop of relevant content created a website that people would visit and visit often. Facebook became the most visited website, with people spending on average thirty-seven minutes on the site every day.[121] However, add on Instagram and WhatsApp— two platforms now owned by Facebook—and Facebook balloons to taking over our lives for more than an hour each day.

Big thinkers can adopt the viral mental model to purposefully use exponential growth to their benefit. Remember Metcalfe's Law: the power of a network doubles with each user. Every time we're able to add another content-contributing customer, it raises the probability that new users will join the network. Facebook's viral loop was able to grow so much because first, its business model was built on the network law, and second, it pivoted to a mobile model as the world went mobile with the iPhone moment.

The Insta-Moment

Three years after TheFacebook.com launched, the iPhone moment changed mobile computing forever. This moment was a major societal shift to mass mobile digitization. Facebook, consequently, needed to move to a digital app or risk mobile disruption, as its customers were inevitably going mobile.

Fortunately for Facebook, as with many other exponential companies, it was built lean and adaptable. The iPhone moment—

which brought down so many other businesses—provided Facebook with a tsunami of progress that it could surf on. Post-iPhone moment, 98% of Facebook users are on a mobile app now.[122] If Facebook did not ride the tsunami of the mobile wave, it would've been trying to survive off the less than 2% of those who access Facebook from desktop or laptops. This is still a big number, yet it is nothing compared to the influence Facebook has on the world now. With so many millions of new users joining the network thanks to mobile digitization and the iPhone moment, the network's power exploded. This mobilization only sped up Facebook's viral loop as now it was easy to connect to people on the go.

The faster viral loop made Facebook even more instantaneous. This timeliness resulted in even greater relevancy. Users were refreshing their Facebook web browser page (before the iPhone moment) to get relevant content. But with the app, the refresh was instant and almost never-ending. iPhones had cameras, so immediately uploaded content kept everyone informed of every move. So many people were plugged in and sharing content that it was overflowing.

The content became so abundant that Facebook was starting to fade for its users. The solution was adjustments to how people see algorithms, now causing issues as Facebook filters content. This filtering caused Facebook to only show users content that they liked and expected to see, creating a one-sided story with no objectivity. Unfortunately, users are now caught in a polarized view of the world with mini hits of dopamine from content they already expect to see. The art of forming new connections in the brain or new thought patterns from learning is unlikely as Facebook has made it easy for our brains to accept what is in our feed already. Others that like to see things they do not agree with get plenty of that in their feed.

Then in 2012, Facebook acquired Instagram for $1 billion dollars. Since the acquisition, Instagram absorbed Facebook's viral loop and has grown as powerful—if not more so—than its parent company. According to Facebook, in 2020, more than 500 million Instagram accounts are active every day, and over one billion accounts are active every month.[123] In hindsight, Facebook's $1 billion acquisition price for Instagram in 2012 was a great bargain for a company that had twelve employees. After that, Facebook acquired WhatsApp. WhatsApp is a messaging app that Facebook bought in 2015 for $19 billion. It's the world's most popular messaging app with over two billion users in 2020. This purchase was to both grow and alleviate the pressure Facebook was under with its own viral loop.

Humans struggled to adapt to a viral world. New content was pouring out at such a fast rate that it was impossible to fact check it all, and news shifted as special interest groups engaged in fake news. Major election disruption was traced to Russian Facebook meddling in the 2016 presidential election. Society stopped believing in facts and science. Users exaggerated their content to make their lives seem more desirable, to chase likes and shares. The "influencers," catering to their audiences with various trends to get "likes," arrived to convince the rest of us that our lives were somehow inferior. Young social media users were left with skewed perceptions of reality, causing brutal self-esteem issues and social network depression.

Facebook is largely unregulated, and as a result, the network is held responsible (if unfairly) for how humans grapple with accelerating change and information overload. Facebook does need to decide if it filters content and does not censor untruthful or socially acceptable content. Essentially, it needs to find where it draws the line. Over time, artificial intelligence (AI) will hopefully be able to better assist Facebook in weeding out fake news, but Facebook will first need to accept that it has a role to play in regulating its content.

This is what happens when a network gets too powerful for its users to handle, and if it was not Facebook, another platform would've filled the void. In July 2020, Facebook is dealing with major advertisers like Unilever, Verizon, Coca-Cola, Microsoft, and more than 750 other major brands pulling their spend from the platform until it stops promoting ads that incite discrimination, bias, and/or hate. The world's growing social consciousness led by brands will help us define a more fair and equitable future for all. Facebook will have to find a viewpoint quickly.

Ultimately, the viral loop that we have learned from Facebook will be monumentally good for mankind. Until then, there will be growing pains. Truly, it's unrealistic to expect that humans will be able to adapt to technology at the same speed the technology grows, but that's part of the deal.

Design is the New Marketing

The viral loop model that Facebook popularized changed marketing as we know it. Companies shifted from sales focus to engineering focus, as engineers can build the next great viral loop. Now, companies can directly address their viral coefficient to evaluate their growth potential, and marketing is less about the product and more about the user. So, design becomes the new marketing: nearly every future company will need to design an internal media company. This internal media company must be designed to gain users rather than push products. Red Bull may have been the company that invented this, as its internal media company managed to make a sales juggernaut from a poor tasting energy drink through media stunts and sponsorship of extreme sports. Red Bull gives you wings.

This shift makes sense in a world of chaos, spewing more content than ever before. If users are the fuel for the viral loop, then the user base becomes the most important part of the marketing. To get a user's attention, it takes great design and content. The product doesn't matter; what matters is whether users will convince others to hop on the product's bandwagon. When it was first released, Snapchat appeared to be just a better way for users to share nude pictures. It was counterintuitive—it did not save the photos for the user—and at first, it was only users messaging other users. When Snapchat turned down a $2 billion offer from Facebook, it seemed like a squandered opportunity for the Snapchat founders.

Yet Snapchat not only survived, but it also started dominating certain Gen Y and Z segments for communicating and is worth many multiples of what Facebook tendered. That's because Snapchat was viewing the users as the product. As long as users kept returning to Snapchat, making relevant content, and referring new users, Snapchat was growing exponentially. Ever since, there has been a slew of popup tech companies.

Remember Flappy Bird? It was a touch screen game that looked eerily similar to Super Mario World. Flappy Bird had a viral loop going for it when users started getting high scores and daring their friends to best them. It did not matter that the game was a janky, keep-the-bird-afloat game; it was extremely popular. So popular in fact that the creator—a developer from Vietnam making $50,000 per day—took it off the app store after millions of downloads. Dong Nguyen did not see himself as an entrepreneur. He did not want the pressure of users attacking his art and traded it all in for peace of mind.[124]

The viral loop works for the good and the bad. Flappy Bird, Angry Birds, Clash of Clans, Farmville, and Words with Friends were all able to make millions just by getting users to share with their friends, leveraging the global networks that connect us all. None of these games had the depth or sophistication of games that competitors PlayStation and Xbox could offer, but that did not matter. They were free or very low cost, and heck, even grandma was playing Angry Birds and Pocket Poker.

By the same token, the viral loop can be brutal. That wide-open, three-point air-ball? It went viral. It's on video and the human condition will share interesting content. That road rage incident? Went viral. The last second air ball? Viral. Facebook's greatest contribution to the exponential world was not the social media component; it was unleashing the law of networks.

The viral mental model has fundamentally changed both "what" and "how" exponential leaders sell to customers. The product matters significantly less, while the user matters significantly more. The game can be dumb, the drink can taste bad, or the facts can be made up; all that matters is that enough users share it. Because of this, using the viral mental model is a tool of great responsibility for all big thinkers and participants in the exponential theory. What we write on the internet is in ink, not pencil, and the viral loop is what makes that statement matter.

Facebook has some challenges as the endless scroll leads users to compare culture and always measuring up short. Facebook's role in fake news, polarizing views, and meddling in politics have both sides upset. Facebook's censorship of the Rohingya genocide in Burma, role in Pizzagate, Russia's meddling in the 2016 election, and removal of Donald Trump post 2020 Capitol siege allows the world's largest communication platform to play favorites. Zuckerberg's congressional testimonial failed to answer some basic questions, yet it was also misunderstood by unconnected politicians representing a generation completely unfamiliar with the technology.

Nonetheless, the same privacy issues that plague Google users, plague Facebook and a movement to remove Facebook may mean that the company has peaked. If Facebook survives it will need to protect their users' data, be transparent with it, build a more fair and just algorithm to avoid creating even more polarizing views, solve for the endless scroll, address censorship, find better solution for "likes" and compare culture, cancel culture, and work to provide solutions to become a better corporate citizen on behalf of its users.

REFLECTION

Now is all we've got. Be present. In the era of the viral loop, it's possible to go viral in any moment. Further, living in such a digital age makes it more difficult than ever to be present.

- Were you an early adopter, or a resistor of Facebook?
- What were the factors that drew you into the viral loop?
- How do you get, keep, and grow your customers?

Consider Red Bull and Flappy Bird. Both were weak products that were able to succeed because of their marketing-first approach.

- What other products/services exist today have viral loops built into them?
- Could you use an engineering first approach over sales?
- How can you leverage a viral loop to grow your business?

Chapter 9.

Playing the Long Game

"If you double the number of experiments you do per year, you're going to double your inventiveness."
—Jeff Bezos, Amazon

Not Just Another Book Company

Exponential companies like Amazon begin in a shroud of deception. When Amazon launched, did any of us think that an online book retailer would take turns with Google, Apple, and Microsoft as the wealthiest company in the world? Highly doubtful.

Amazon began thinking exponentially, digitizing the model from the start, and they were a tech company from the beginning. It was the tech company that was going to be "Earth's most customer-centric company,"[125] which is a massive transformative purpose. It was going to have the fastest, most complete customer service, and was going to supply goods and services to its customers like no company before it. Amazon just happened to start off selling books, yet later found ways to launch disruption, leverage the viral loop, and arguably played the long game better than any company in history. The structure and culture of Amazon may have been the reason Bezos trades places with Elon Musk to be the richest man on the planet. Bezos created the framework for success and then stepped out of the way.

Amazon's low cost direct-to-consumer model is responsible for the demise of many companies, one of the most notable was Borders. Amazon's digitization demonetized, democratized, and dematerialized the publishing and books industry, and Borders evaporated as people shifted to the bits and bytes online and disrupted the retail experience.

Dematerialization was the first major blow to Borders. A similar effect that Netflix ultimately had on Blockbuster. Amazon had on Borders. The cost of running a Borders bookstore was immense. The stores, on average, were 25,000-square-foot retail spaces, about half the size of a football field.[126] All that space came with inventory, retail staff, constant reorganization of the books, theft, building maintenance, tenant improvements, inventory, clearance sales that led to revenue losses, and other overhead. Much like Netflix, Amazon only needed a website. At first, Amazon did not even need to hold inventory. Borders had a massive inventory they had to carry in their store. Borders superstores housed up to 171,000 book titles.[127] The property needed tremendous space to not only house the books, but also so the staff could organize, access, and sell them easily. Even worse, the books that didn't sell sat there or sold at a loss to make space for new books.

Meanwhile, Amazon was also able to offer nearly every book in the world through dematerialization, not just the books "in-store." Books were housed in warehouses around the country and could be purchased through the website anywhere in the country, not just at the local store (democratize). Amazon has over 3.4 million[128] book titles on-demand, meaning Amazon customers had more titles to choose from at a lower cost (demonetize) and they were rarely sold out. Remember, disruption yields a win for the customer. Amazon took advantage of that disruption and was able to offer an inventory long tail, offering up to 90% more books available online than in-store. Amazon sold bestsellers at 30–50% off to lure customers in and familiarize them with the Amazon e-commerce model.

This created the experience of showrooming, where people would essentially window-shop at Borders or Barnes and Noble. They'd feel the books, peruse, maybe read a few pages, and then leave the store empty-handed only to buy the book later on Amazon. Sometimes, customers would pull up their Amazon app and buy the same book from Amazon while standing in Barnes and Noble—which was awkward at first, but now is a norm. The customer would save money but get the book a day or two later. Amazon dematerialized the bookstore into a website and eventually an app after the iPhone moment turned their opponents into free book browsing.

Further digitizing, Amazon introduced Kindle and digital e-books. E-books were instantly available and abundant, with zero incremental cost, essentially zero storage space, and nearly 100% profit—increasing sales and profits for both the author and Amazon. Now, customers can get an e-book instantly, or with Prime in most urban centers, can get a paperback or hardcover book a few hours later, and in some cases just one hour. It became very clear that Borders was going to be eliminated by Amazon; the clock for Barnes and Noble is a ticking time bomb, likely ignited during COVID-19, as stores across the world closed. Amazon further democratized books by offering Kindle Unlimited, a subscription service for books.

Death of the Shopping Mall

America was once known for its main streets littered with mom-and-pop stores, its strip malls to satisfy nearly every delight, and its shopping malls to escape from the real world. Malls became sprawling mini cities, filled every day of the week with teenagers, families, friends, and the smell of movie popcorn from theatres, and Cinnabon's or Sbarro Pizza from the food court. Shopping malls provided communities with franchises and vendors that brought products from across the globe to malls everywhere in the country and around the world. Malls represent classic Americana: regardless of the region, they were filled with the same food courts, department stores, brands, and blockbuster movie premieres pulling in consumers every weekend. They were a powerful machine in the consumer-driven Western world.

Shopping malls had previously disrupted main street shops, mom-and-pop stores, and the country store as they brought cheaper (demonetized) products from coast to coast and made them accessible to everyone, even in rural America, through regional malls (democratized).

Amazon's massive disruptive power of digitization began with just books, soon after electronics, but has now shifted to retail in general. Now, Amazon threatens to wipe out the retail industry as we know it. It has already changed retail forever.

Soon, Amazon (the most customer-centric company on Earth) started offering the same products, for less (demonetize), able to be delivered everywhere (democratize), and created a better customer service experience in the process. In fact, they would even lose money on products like books and electronics[129] to gain customers, providing a business model that increased customer acquisition and retraining shoppers to shop online.

The customer stopped buying in the malls and started show-rooming, the same as they did at Borders. Consumers visited malls and went into stores, checked out the products, heard the pitches from the sales staff, but then left. They went home and bought whatever product they were interested in online for a cheaper price. The stores are full, but nobody is buying anything.

The average shopping malls—anchored by department stores like JCPenney, Sears, Kmart, Bloomingdale's, Nordstrom, and Neiman Marcus—were toast. It didn't matter if their customers were rich or poor, they were beginning to buy online. The physical location of the mall, which used to be an asset, quickly became a disadvantage. In fact, the physical malls became liabilities as many retail stores have begun to disappear, becoming gyms, restaurants, swap meets, fresh markets, or now indoor playgrounds.

High-end malls were the only real survivors of Amazon's shift to retail, spared only because they provided customers direct access to more exclusive brands. Brands like Apple, Lululemon, Coach, and Louis Vuitton pivoted to direct experience with their customers, building physical and digital stores exclusive to their brand. Consumers could experience the products, and the businesses didn't care if they purchased online or in the store, because they had cut out the middleman. This was a survivable business model for the digital age. Apple proved this model, recreating the retail experience and yielding more dollars per square foot than any other retailer in history.[130] Amazon would follow suit acquiring Whole Foods, launching Amazon Books, and now Amazon Go to disrupt the convenience space market. Meanwhile, brands that didn't have their own store were losing margin when their products had to be sold in electronic stores, grocery stores, department stores, or worse yet, Amazon. Traditional players with no digital strategy were left behind and became irrelevant to baby boomers and millennials alike.

Things looked bleak for non-brand specific stores, like electronics store Circuit City, which went from strip mall staple to extinct. The inevitable digitization of their business was ignored by the executives, another classic example of the deceptive phase of the 6Ds. Soon, the rest of the strip malls and shopping malls followed suit and gave way to their own heavy inventories and high retail costs, while Amazon could warehouse 100x mall inventory and still sell it at prices that undercut mall stores.

Herein lies the most fundamental truth about change and disruption: it is a cycle. When something goes up, something else must come down. Digitization brought the stores down with a heavy, invisible hand. Now, consumers look to their smartphones to purchase products first and go to the mall as a last resort. RIP Sears.

Hey Alexa...

In Jeff Bezos's 1997 shareholder letter, he outlined Amazon's focus: to be the world's most customer-centric company.[131] Now, over twenty-three years later, in the COVID-19 global pandemic, it's apparent that his goal has been realized. When all the other stores closed and businesses shuttered, Amazon was still there, serving the customers. Amazon's commitment to its customers was quite literally saving lives, as those at risk of becoming sick could truly quarantine with Amazon's help. Further, Amazon was able to stay open as an essential business that saved hundreds of thousands of jobs and helped prop up an economy suffering the highest unemployment rates since the Great Depression. Amazon was the most customer-centric company in the world during the pandemic.

Much like Domino's and Starbucks became tech companies that sell pizza or coffee, Amazon is a tech company that sells customer service. Putting the customer first means making products and services available faster, cheaper, and easier. When Amazon puts the customer first, everything it does revolves around relieving pains and providing gains to its customers, which is ultimately their flagship product—customer service.

How can we make this faster, cheaper, and easier?

This question is in fact a multi-pronged question of disruption: How can we dematerialize, demonetize, and democratize? This is always in the customer's interest, but it's also very disruptive. So, while Amazon was building the most customer-centric company in the world, it was disrupting itself as well as the competition. Through disruption, the customer wins, or the company dies.

As Amazon disrupted itself, it continually improved the customer experience. For example, take the improved customer service of two-day delivery. This was an expensive bet for Amazon because it meant higher delivery costs and ate into any potential profits at the time. Yet Amazon continued to disrupt itself even more. What would customers love more than two-day delivery? Even faster delivery. In some areas, Amazon now offers one-hour delivery through its Prime service. Amazon took the time and the money to set up its own two-day delivery guarantee, just to go and disrupt it again. Soon, fleets of autonomous drones will deliver packages from Amazon warehouses and leave them in our backyards, potentially instantaneously.

Digitization provides Amazon customers way more than just fast delivery. Now, Amazon can accurately predict product fulfillment based on customer data and advanced algorithms. With its predictive AI, Amazon knows what customers want before they do. Therefore, Amazon amasses a massive marketing weapon, given its customer success. "Amazon always knows what I need."

Amazon's flagship product, Alexa, is the epitome of customer service and only something an exponential technology company could launch. Alexa continues to learn skills and improve integration with the rest of Amazon's exponential technologies, like AI, machine learning, robotics, and automation among others. Alexa now has many devices—integrated into the TV, car, convenience store, pharmacy, mobile phone, and at every point of sale—enabling Amazon to deliver its standard of customer service anywhere. The question for the future is this: Will Alexa be the only employee left standing as "she" becomes the best customer service representative in the world?

Obviously, Amazon's superior customer service results in more customers and deeper relationships. Amazon has set the bar for customer experience so high that it has become the new standard. As consumers shift online to purchase everything, Amazon continues to add new customers. When it acquires another customer, it increases the strength of its gravitational pull, and it makes its network exponentially stronger. The more people join the network, the more powerful the benefits for customers become. Amazon can coordinate delivery batches and optimize efficiencies.

While Amazon's network grew, so did its marketplace. The Amazon third-party marketplace opened the doors for thousands of companies and entrepreneurs to sell their products using Amazon's platform. Amazon had already spent time cultivating its user base. Much like a huge whale in the ocean, many smaller companies attached themselves to Amazon and followed it to the feeding grounds. Companies have been presented with a choice: find the customers on their own, or team up with Amazon and let Amazon bring the customers to them.

The Amazon marketplace created millions of jobs and opportunities for small business owners. Amazon transformed from a company to a whole economy of its own, all the while still improving its premium customer service. Amazon continued to expand its product offerings because of its inventory management abilities. It allowed competitors to sell the same goods through its marketplace but took a piece of the action to do so. The Amazon app became a platform that connected producers and consumers instantly (much like Uber and Airbnb) in a way that was not possible before.

The customer first/disruption mindset makes Amazon a threat to nearly every industry. With its size, technology, and infrastructure, Amazon can effortlessly enter and transform large industries overnight. Suddenly, Amazon starts to follow its customer and takes over other industries, as the customer demands the same experience that Amazon delivers in other areas of their lives.

Most recently, Amazon acquired PillPack and consequently sent shockwaves—specifically, a collective 27% decline in industry stocks—through their competitors, a total loss of $11 billion dollars of value overnight.[132] With its effective supply chain, Amazon has entered the colossal-sized industry, soon to potentially eliminate the Walgreens, Rite Aid, and Walmart pharmacies on every corner. Even CVS, currently the largest U.S. pharmacy, is no match for Amazon and the Prime machine.

When Amazon acquired Whole Foods for $13.4 billion, its stock growth helped Amazon bridge the last mile into the trillion-dollar club. Now, the grocery industry is set to be disrupted.

Amazon was able to sustain its plan of disruption because of its goal from 1997: to be Earth's most customer-centric company. Internally, that required a significant shift in how business should be done. To improve the customer experience, Amazon continued to invest in shrinking margins, which is the exact opposite of many other companies' strategies.

The customer-first model is a long-term approach that exponential leaders can adopt if they are willing to also rely on innovation and patience. While the contrarian model took a couple of decades to play out, Bezos's focus on tech, customers, innovation, and patience created one of the world's most valuable companies.

The Long Game

Amazon is the largest internet company by revenue, the second-largest employer in the United States only to Walmart and rotates with Apple, Microsoft, and Google as the world's most valuable company. It's also one of the most innovative companies in the world. Bezos famously said, "We've had three big ideas at Amazon that we've stuck with for eighteen years, and they're the reason we're successful: Put the customer first. Invent. And be patient."[133]

These big three ideas that Amazon follows are chronological. To put customers first is to disrupt. To disrupt, Amazon must innovate. However, to see these innovations pay off, it must be patient. The combination of these ideas culminates in Bezos's philosophy and is a key component of the exponential theory: the long game.

Bezos has been playing the long game since the beginning of Amazon when he was peddling books online. Imagine the doubt most entrepreneurs would have had along the way. Leaders stay focused on their long-term vision, even if others are not able to see it. Bezos knew that what he was doing would inevitably make Amazon's customer service superior, although the disruption would take some time to actualize.

The first step of the long-term vision is the "Day 1" culture that Amazon has established. It asks each employee to treat every day as if it were day one. The idea is simple: on the first day of a job, school, or new adventure, there is an intoxicating excitement. This excitement produces a greater amount of brain functioning, which literally yields creativity. Jeff Bezos named his office building Day 1, and that's because of how he views Day 2: "Day 2 is stasis. Followed by irrelevance. Followed by excruciating, painful decline. Followed by death. And that is why it is always Day 1."[134] When stasis takes over, the lack of passion to put the customer first dies and so does the innovation and creativity behind it.

Since it's always Day 1, every process has the same first step-focus on the customer. This is also called inverse thinking and leverages design thinking, where we start with the customer and work backward. When Amazon identifies a customer pain or a potential customer gain, it writes a mock internal press release to announce its solution. Next, it creates a user manual that centers around its customers, and the jobs-to-be-done. Then the solution is made. Amazon finishes its process on the product or service, which is where most of its competition starts. However, with the design thinking model, it takes on the customer's journey just as the customer would experience it, by reading the press release and the user's manual, and then using the product. With this process, it's impossible to not put the customer first, which sets Amazon up for success in the innovation stage.

Bezos empowers Amazon's employees to experiment to encourage innovation. Once Amazon's innovative employees have the freedom to invent, they can truly create solutions that benefit the customer from any job in the building. Promising to give employees a fair chance to see their solution play out only fuels the innovation machine.

There's no better example of Amazon's innovation and patience than its "two-pizza teams." The two-pizza teams are intimate groups of builders that can be fed by no more than two-pizzas. They're empowered with the freedom to invent, experiment, and wait. Amazon's more than ten thousand two-pizza teams have been responsible for several profound Amazon projects, including Alexa, Kindle, and the Fire TV Stick.

Ten thousand teams seem aggressive, but it's well rooted in theory. Malcolm Gladwell popularized the rule of ten thousand hours in his book, *Outliers*.[135] The idea is that you need ten thousand hours of deliberate practice to become an expert in your field. Michael Simmons, a mental model practitioner, used this idea to create the ten thousand experiment rule: "Deliberate experimentation is more important than deliberate practice in a rapidly changing world."[136]

According to folklore, it took Thomas Edison ten thousand experiments to invent the light bulb. Dyson allegedly invented his high suction vacuum cleaner after six thousand experiments. This absolutely clarifies that experimentation is a key factor in the success of innovation, and justifies Amazon supporting ten thousand experiments at any time.

The two-pizza teams are fast and agile, and foster ownership and autonomy. When an employee can make decisions, they are going to be a lot more productive. The ownership allows them to stand behind their idea, vouch for it, and explain how their solution puts the customers first. Employee ownership empowers employees to fight for their projects but also allows the teams to fail without fear of getting ostracized. The Amazon Fire Phone—a product of a two-pizza team—was probably the biggest flop Amazon has had to date. However, the team celebrated its failures and part of the same team that flopped with the Fire Phone went on to help develop Alexa, likely the biggest success to date, and seemingly growing faster and smarter than Apple's Siri, Microsoft's Cortana, or the Google Assistant.

This intense number of fast experiments is useful in a world where organizations need to stay lean and agile. Making small, incremental improvements will translate into a massive increase to the bottom line. Professional athletes make small improvements every day and are dramatically better at the end of the offseason. That's because small quick wins compound into exponential results over time, while still maintaining low risk. The key is to continually evolve and adapt like it's the first day.

Plus, there's always the chance that one of those experiments hits big. Amazon struck gold when it wasn't even looking for it by putting the customer first, inventing, and being patient. Amazon Web Services (AWS) was a system that Amazon built internally to power its own service. This was Bezos's understanding that Amazon needed to compete and win as a tech company, not just an e-commerce company. It was a necessary mindset to execute Amazon functions and deliver customer value, and AWS was the result. Amazon executives didn't consider the potential power of AWS if it were to become external, rather than internal.

Now, the commercialized Amazon Web Services drives a significant chunk of Amazon's bottom-line profit. AWS is the pay-as-you-go cloud platform that fully integrates business applications for developers, companies, and governments alike. Amazon launched AWS to help scale its business with speed, and now it can offer the same tool to every business.

Amazon has now created more than two hundred services from computing, storage, networking, database, analytics, application services, mobile, development tools, and IoT tools. According to Synergy Group, AWS owns 33% of all cloud services, more than the next three competitors combined.[137] Amazon Web Services became so big that eventually, Amazon was able to power many other brands to offer their own customers the same thing Amazon offers its customers: exponential benefits.

As other businesses use the same technology stack as Amazon, the reach of the company continues to expand and touch nearly every company in the world in some way. Inevitably, everything could run with or through Amazon—which, as we've pointed out, is a good thing for the consumers—because Amazon's focus will make the world cheaper, faster, and easier. Leaders can apply the same mental models of patience, innovation, and customer first; above all in their own pursuit of exponential growth, regardless of their industry, pursuits, or talents. After all, wasn't Amazon just another eCommerce book company when it started?

From the employee-less checkout at Amazon Go convenience stores to the brick-and-mortar retail chain Amazon Books popping up in the surviving malls, the outlook for current competitors is bleak, as customers will be able to experience, shop, and pick up goods conveniently using Amazon. With its acquisition of Whole Foods, Amazon can provide new grocery services in nearly every market in America. The data from Whole Foods complemented the data from Amazon Prime, creating exponential opportunities in the largest retail industry: grocery. Amazon continues to seek every last remnant to control the showroom and the back end to improve the experience for the customers.

So, while Amazon was the tech company that sold customer service, it has disrupted many industries with its continuous transformation. Alexa, Prime, and the countless other flagship products that Amazon offers are changing how customers live in the world, and what they demand from the rest of the businesses they interact with. Amazon set the bar so high it seems that it could run everybody out of business because its customer experience is unmatched. Yet, they need to address a slew of issues with their workforce, come to terms or overcome the need for unions, and continue to improve as nearly every exponential company in the world is creating an MVP (minimum viable product) to compete with some part of their business. Let's take a closer look at how one of our greatest innovator's approaches executing on an MVP.

REFLECTION

The journey is the reward. At Amazon, Day One is every day. Day Two is stasis.

- How can you shift your business to focus on the long game?
- How can you focus your company on a purpose everyday?
- Disruption is inevitable, what are your contingency plans?
- How can you improve your customer service with technology?

Chapter 10

Executing the MVP

*"When something is important enough, you do it
even if the odds are not in your favor."*
—Elon Musk

The Exponential Leader

There's a legendary story that after Elon Musk sold PayPal, he netted $180 million.[138] He was rich beyond most people's wildest dreams. Immediately, Musk invested all the money he made into three of his companies—$100 million into SpaceX, $70 million into Tesla, and $10 million into SolarCity. Only after his major investment did Musk realize he was short on rent. The same day he made $180 million, he had to call a friend and borrow money for rent.[139]

How can someone be that crazy to take everything as he was set for life, and risk it all? Elon Musk thinks differently. He is deeply rooted in exponential theory and the clearest example of big thinking in our lifetime.

On the surface, it's ridiculous. Surely, he could've saved some money for his rent. However, Musk's companies are all ExOs. They were all still floating around the second stage of the exponential curve, the deception stage, and needed the resources to grow. Musk, the big thinker he is, was probably one of the only people at the time who knew such an investment would pay off. He believed in each of these companies when everyone doubted him and his ability to do what he has done. He had the vision, understanding, clarity, and agility to make it happen.

These three major companies—among the handful of others Musk has created—are all home runs and have either disrupted their industries or replaced them. Their exponential technologies will all fundamentally change the way we live life, while demonetizing, dematerializing, and democratizing the world around us. Tesla will eventually eliminate driving. SpaceX will colonize other planets. SolarCity (now part of Tesla) will supply the universe with near free, infinite clean renewable power. It would be a remarkable life to have founded and own any one of these companies. Elon Musk founded and owns all three, and he didn't stop there.

Musk's relentless focus on exponential technology has led him to disrupt many industries. He's also disrupted global payments and online payments with PayPal; fast transit with Hyperloop; artificial intelligence with OpenAI; and tunnel construction with The Boring Company.

This focus on exponential technology provides Musk with entirely different ways of solving problems. With Tesla, Musk did not set out to make the best electric car; he set out to make the best, most powerful battery in the world. Musk knew the problem he needed to solve was not a better Prius, but a better battery. With the most powerful battery in the world, he would be able to make the best electric car. But he also changed how we think about energy. Tesla isn't a car company, it's an energy company; its MTP is "to accelerate the world's transition to sustainable energy."[140]

Being an energy company instead of a car company makes Tesla much more disruptive. It simultaneously disrupted both auto competitors and fuel competitors along the way. Other exponential technologies—in addition to the battery Musk bundled into Tesla—included autonomous driving, software updating, and solar technology. This layering of technology has demonetized, dematerialized, and democratized the world faster than any other company. Now making Tesla more valuable than all other automobile companies combined.

With so much technology rolled into one, the stages of disruption are multifold. For example, Tesla's demonetization surged with the battery, solar, software, and autonomous technologies. The world's most powerful battery continues to become cheaper to make, so it's cheaper to sell to the customer. The battery eliminates the need for gas and uses much cheaper (and cleaner) electricity. Soon, the ability to solar charge will eliminate the electricity charging cost, too.

The software updating allows Tesla owners to download newer versions of the car, continuously improving the Tesla experience, at a minimal expense to the consumer. Eventually, when autonomous vehicles take over the road, the Tesla vehicle will moonlight as a self-driving taxi, making money for the Tesla owner when it'd otherwise be unused.

Tesla battery technology is dematerialized as it improves and gets smaller. Potentially, Tesla will dematerialize solar technology into the body of a car, or a windshield, dematerializing the huge solar panels of the past needed to create enough energy to make an impact. Competing automaker Fisker has already brought solar back into the electric car.[141] When solar and battery technology do replace gas, they will dematerialize the millions of gas stations in the world and there will be no need for Tesla Superchargers. Now, Tesla can slap solar panels and a battery on an exterior of a house the size of a fridge that can power nearly the whole house, localizing power.

Finally, all these exponential technologies are democratizing. As the battery, autonomous, and solar technologies get dematerialized and demonetized, they become available to the masses. It's quite possible that eventually, Musk will create the new Model T, the car everybody will have. A truly disruptive model would be a membership model, allowing unlimited access to a Tesla.

When Musk was dreaming up Tesla and thinking big, he saw the future disruption Tesla would create. He even wrote about this plan in detail in a 2006 blog post, titled "The Secret Tesla Motors Master Plan (just between you and me)." The stages of disruption are woven throughout it.

Deception: "When someone buys the Tesla Roadster sports car, they are actually helping pay for the development of the lower-cost family car." [142]

Demonetization: "The strategy of Tesla is to enter at the high end of the market, where customers are prepared to pay a premium, and then drive down the market as fast as possible to higher unit volume and lower prices with each successive model."[143]

Democratization: The Model 3 rolls out and creates the first mass adopted electric car.

In 2006, Musk outlined all the steps of disruption that Tesla was going to take. The end result, as he sees it, is that Tesla owners will " . . . be putting more energy back into the system than [Tesla owners] consume in transportation!" All this disruption at the hand of an electric car, made possible by the hyper-focus on the MVP.

Not Another Prius

The minimum viable product (MVP) is the initial prototype that entrepreneurs use to showcase how they will deliver their unique value proposition. It's critical to not only explain the idea but also gauge customer interest and gather any feedback. It's a particularly important process for big thinkers because it forces us to change how we present and explain our ideas. Leaders don't fret that they have dreamed something too big to build, because they break it down to the MVP first.

The successful MVP must walk customers through the whole idea, addressing any skepticism. The deceptive phase on the curve of disruption tricks customers and competitors because the cost of the exponential technology in the early stage is enormous, and the value of the technology isn't justified. So, how can visionaries create exponential MVPs?

The Tesla Roadster is the prime example of an exponential technology's MVP. The two impediments that exponential technologies pose to MVPs are the cost and the lack of perceived value. So, to attack both of those problems, Musk built an expensive car that was faster than any other car on the road. The high price allowed for the cars to be built while the battery technology was still so expensive. Building the fastest car on the road helped customers see the value in the technology. Musk was not pitching customers an electric car; he was pitching them the fastest car in the world. He did this by focusing on creating the best battery.

The creator of the Lean Canvas, Author of *Running Lean* and *Scaling Lean*, Ash Maurya calls the Tesla Roadster the "Wizard of Oz MVP."[144] Again treating Tesla as an energy company and not a car company, Musk set out to build the battery first, and the car second. As a result, Tesla did not even bother designing anything besides the battery for its MVP. Instead, it licensed the Lotus Elise body to serve as the vehicle to deliver the battery. This allowed them to skip the whole car design and manufacturing design process. The result, Ash Maurya notes, was a Tesla Roadster that "they got to market with a road-ready vehicle in under three years— which is light speed compared to other car companies."[145] Musk continues to disrupt Tesla itself, and now it is the most valuable car company in the world.[146]

The MVP is Musk's best ability. The Tesla Roadster highlighted his ability to view a problem differently—not build the best electric car but build the best battery. The partnership with Lotus serves, too, as another indication of Musk's focus. The technology was the priority, and the rest was just filler.

Another legendary Musk MVP story: In December 2016, while stuck in traffic, Musk tweeted "[I] am going to build a tunnel boring machine and just start digging . . . "[147] Doesn't get much more minimal than that. Subsequently, Musk created The Boring Company, to introduce society to exponential construction and tunnels. In just two years, The Boring Company had already begun—or had approved plans—to begin construction in major U.S. cities like Baltimore, Chicago, and Los Angeles. This almost flippant company idea, born because Musk was frustrated with traffic, started with a simple way to show value: dig.

Just like how Tesla isn't a car company but is rather an energy company, SpaceX isn't a spaceship company, it's a transportation company. But of course, there will be skepticism because of the cost and perceived value. How can customers see the value of a travel company like SpaceX if they can't actually travel in space now?

SpaceX's first MVP addressed travel implications on Earth. Currently, a direct flight from New York to Shanghai is about eighteen hours (though it could take days with connections). In the near future, SpaceX proposes that its point-to-point rocket transportation would take that eighteen-hour commute and whittle it down to thirty-nine minutes.[148] That's right, we could get from Times Square to Shanghai in less time than it takes to watch an episode of our favorite TV show. Another MVP for this project was the reusable rocket. SpaceX launched Falcon 9 and landed vertically in 2015, enabling it to be reused on future missions. What was previously called impossible has now been done many times by SpaceX. Musk said he was going to make a reusable rocket to decrease the price of space travel by 10x (demonetization) and well, he did it. SpaceX focused on the technology that will get humans to space, like how Tesla focused on the battery. Instead of car and spaceship companies, they're energy and transportation companies. This prompts leaders to ask, how do we expand our goals to the size of a whole industry?

Mars Shots (Beyond Moon Shots)

Through the different types of Musk's companies, it's clear that his emphasis on exponential technologies is a stark differentiator. In Musk's case, Mars Shots put the goal out there so far, even if he fails, he has succeeded. We argue that focusing on technology is a requirement for the exponential theory but also for thinking big:

- It changes how they view the problem (think: building the battery, not the car).
- It allows the visionary to see along the exponential curve and into the future.

Viewing the problem differently and along the exponential curve, Musk created a satellite project within SpaceX called Starlink. Starlink is an initiative that found a way to make thousands of low-cost, low-Earth orbit (LEO) satellites that when launched into space can provide high-speed internet connectivity to every corner of the Earth. Surely, Starlink will become one of the major catalysts for digitization and mass access.

Musk seems hell-bent on removing traffic from our world with a variety of exponential technologies. The Hyperloop, similar to the bullet train, is high-speed transportation that runs on air. A bullet train has hyper-powerful magnets that suspend the train above the track, reducing air friction and allowing for very high speeds. The Hyperloop functions in a semi-vacuum, so there is minimal air resistance. Just introducing this technology to the public has allowed others to think about travel from major cities—like San Francisco to LA, or D.C. to Baltimore—in minutes instead of hours.[149]

Furthering the public's acceptance of exponential technologies, Musk set out to tackle artificial intelligence, from concerns about the unknown ethical future of AI. In late 2015, Musk created a nonprofit organization called OpenAI. Its key mission is to develop artificial intelligence in a safe and beneficial way for society. OpenAI is building highly autonomous systems that outperform humans at most economically valuable work. The goal is to benefit all of humanity, yet not have AI robots take over.

When a leader solves problems with technology along the exponential curve, like Starlink, Hyperloop, or OpenAI, they take Mars Shots. Moon Shots are ideas that shoot for the moon, Mars Shots shoot beyond the moon to Mars. With SpaceX, Musk seems out of his mind—or is he? The initial (and still current) goal for SpaceX is to colonize Mars. Musk wants to put humans on the red planet because as he has aggressively argued, the Earth has the potential to become uninhabitable. Musk argues that since the world is dependent on fossil fuels—a finite source—getting the world to go electric with Tesla and SolarCity is Plan A. Plan B is to board SpaceX life "ships" to Mars.

In the quest for the ability to live on Mars (Musk says he's eyeing a colony of eighty thousand by 2040),[150] SpaceX has made some very important technological breakthroughs. NASA engaged SpaceX to shuttle astronauts between the International Space Station and Earth. SpaceX delivered and brought home astronauts for the first time in 2020, privatizing space for the first time.

Finally, SpaceX has its eyes set on asteroids. Asteroids—particularly the ones in between Jupiter and Mars—contain some of the most precious and valuable metals in the universe. This asteroid field alone harbors enough wealth that if dispersed to every person on Earth, would make everyone a billionaire.[151]

Asteroid mining could very well make Musk the first individual multi-trillionaire. There are trillion-dollar companies, but in the past, it seemed impossible for a single person to be worth as much as Google, Apple, Amazon, or Microsoft. What would be more surprising: Musk becoming a trillionaire, or Musk colonizing Mars? Maybe, with the emphasis on exponential technologies, the MVP, and Mars Shots, it's possible after all? Exponential theory has proven it has no bounds. Think big, make small bets, and keep innovating. Musk's mindset is helping many other entrepreneurs set their goals higher as many of his ideas appeared to be delusional, until he proved the naysayers wrong. Musk is a single man accelerator impacting every industry he sets his mind to-the full embodiment of exponential theory.

REFLECTION

Enjoy the process. Elon Musk and Tesla didn't launch a car company, they focused on solving a battery problem. His ability to focus on the specific problem enhanced his chances to solve the problem.

- What problems in your business could launch a new MVP?
- What exponential technologies can you apply to your business model?
- What are some big goals for your company?
- What can you innovate?

Chapter 11.

Accelerating Innovation

*"Because the world is changing, we can never assume
that the way we have done things in the past
is adequate for the future."*
—Yvon Chouinard

Jumping to Hyperdrive

Somewhere in the Yucca Mountains of Nevada, near Groom Lake sits a top-secret US Air Force base. Built in the 1950s, the base, shrouded in secrecy, has been the linchpin of dozens of conspiracy theories. It is a military test center in the desert that the CIA didn't even publicly acknowledge existed until 2013. Though we (still) don't know anything specific about what they do at Area 51, the idea of setting up a top-secret lab outside of headquarters and day-to-day operations is a model we have seen repeated in many industries. Apple, a company that continues to thrive on secrecy and launch unexpected ideas, has its own Area 51 called the Pirate Ship.

Apple's Pirate Ship, complete with its own pirate flag, started when Steve Jobs hand-picked 20 people to move to Texaco Towers to create the then top-secret product to revitalize a dying brand, the Macintosh. Jobs famously said, "It's more fun to be a pirate, than join the Navy."[152] As we've explored Apple's product development engine, this secret nature of their innovation is a major marketing tool. When the media speculates on what Apple is working on next, they're creating billions in free advertising for Apple. What could Apple be developing next, possibly the iCar?

One thing is certain: having a top-secret innovation lab is one of the only ways to pull off that kind of confidentiality and focus. It all started in the 1940s when Lockheed Martin built a jet fighter in 143 days. They were able to do this because they had created a first of its kind innovation lab called Skunk Works where they could hyper-focus on critical projects, while avoiding the bureaucracy and red tape. Skunk Works set the precedent, and innovation labs then expanded beyond the military industry into every other industry. These labs were largely responsible for the industrial revolution.

As organizations add layers of leadership, they create barriers to protect themselves from change. Innovation dies when it challenges the core business. Innovation requires a long-term commitment of both time and resources that companies have had a hard time accepting the risk to reward on such an investment. This is the direct conflict of small thinking vs big thinking. So, when everyone in corporate headquarters has a job responsibility that does not directly benefit from innovation's success, they don't support it. They choose to protect the people, products, and sales of their current business at all costs, even at the potential demise of the company.

While companies struggle with innovating at headquarters, the cost to launch a startup has plummeted and sped up at the same time, enabling a new way to accelerate innovation and put pressure on everyone to jump to hyperdrive. Startups move at light speed compared to companies which it is one reason most exponential startups get acquired before reaching IPO.

As Marc Andreessen claimed software is eating the world, digitization, along with hardware standardization, open-source software, and the cloud, have created a technology stack that has lowered the barriers to entry for everyone. The cost of launching a startup went from an average of $5 million in 1995 to less than $500 today. This 99.9% reduction in cost and time to market is an incomprehensible improvement, leveling the playing field and democratizing startups, entrepreneurship, and innovation. The massive amounts of power we each have with exponential technologies, the internet, and our connected networks, empowers all of us to disrupt the world around us. We all carry more computing power in our hand than NASA had when they put a man on the moon.[153] The democratization of technology has made it easier than ever to solve everyday problems, especially when nearly everyone carries that technology in their pocket everywhere they go. Human collective brain power is stronger than ever, and every generation will solve problems significantly faster than the previous one. As each generation moves faster, the key to leadership and success in the future is developing a growth mindset, as we have examined innovation is the key to our survival. We can no longer do things the same way as we have always done. We must reimagine everything.

So, as companies struggle to protect innovation inside the company and startups innovate faster and faster, companies are moving innovation out of the building. They have begun to innovate on the edge of the company, as they are starting to learn to do it outside of corporate headquarters. The importance of innovation has led nearly every company to invest in its own Accelerator or participate in other Accelerators like Y-Combinator, 500 Startups or TechStars. More innovative companies have launched their own internal accelerators outside of headquarters, such as Google X (now known as X), Xerox PARC, Amazon Lab126, Boeing Phantom Works, Raytheon's Bike Shop, DuPont's Experiment Station, Ford's Special Vehicle Station, and Nike's Innovation Kitchen. Each one of these companies has realized how critical innovation is in competing and pivoting their business model, as business today is constantly shifting the underlying value proposition. As disruption forces everything to change, innovation is the only antidote. Disrupt or be disrupted.

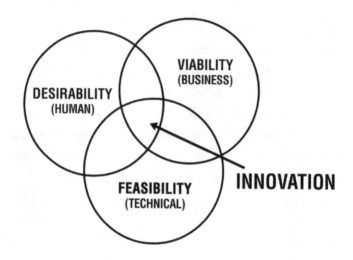

The ability to commercialize innovation is at the intersection of desirability, feasibility, and viability. However, the only way to determine if an idea is desirable, feasible, and viable is to continually test it against assumptions. The faster we iterate the more likely we are to succeed. One way to test iteratively is to use design thinking, a methodology cooked up by IDEO to quickly iterate on ideas. Design thinking is a systemic problem-solving approach focused on experimenting, rather than planning. The goal is validating assumptions, early and often, empowering companies and startups to prioritize ideas and execute, prototype, and create maximum customer value in the process. It also lowers the cost, as decisions are made on evidence and feedback, not hunches or intuition. Design thinking can validate if the problem is one worth targeting and forecast if there is customer value at the end of the tunnel, or if resources are being wasted.

Walmart was a notable example of a company that struggled to innovate online even though it dominated the brick-and-mortar. Walmart attempted to launch an eCommerce platform several times but kept bringing it back to the headquarters too quickly.

Each time Walmart brought it back before it was ready, executives with unaligned goals squashed it. Walmart eventually figured it out and now has a thriving eCommerce business model. It was able to balance the eCommerce business and its brick-and-mortar businesses by treating them as two separate entities. It built an eCommerce business with an external reporting structure and set specific goals that were separate from the main brick-and-mortar business. Letting these two businesses operate side-by-side in parallel is how Walmart was able to finally weave together a disruptive eCommerce business while continuing to run its brick-and-mortar juggernaut. Walmart further bought the online retailer Jet.com to gain ground on Amazon.

IKEA invested in SPACE10, a Copenhagen research and design lab to test new ideas, iterate, and launch new products. SPACE10 is on a mission to create a better everyday life for people and the planet. The lab has begun to ask big questions like how to design the city of the future, redefine technology in the home, create sustainable and affordable homes, write a cookbook for future food, develop a vision of clean energy, and explore the driverless future. Investing in SPACE10 means IKEA can start testing solutions to these major future questions and reimagine its own future, without the burden of managing within its bureaucracy. This is forcing it to move faster.

Accelerators have become their own industry as they move out of the corporate headquarters and into creative spaces made to collaborate and innovate. Accelerators attack specific problems, geographies, customers or industries and provide the same platform Area 51 and Lockheed did to innovate starting nearly 80 years ago. Top accelerators like Y Combinator invest in a startup or product, provide guidance, focus on identifying a worthy problem-solution, iterate from customer feedback, create a minimum viable product, find the product-market fit, launch, accelerate the growth, and scale in weeks instead of years. Accelerators have become highly competitive as they democratize innovation, offering a platform for anyone with a big enough idea and the passion and purpose to solve it. The Y Combinator Accelerator, for example, accepts about 3% of its applicants. For comparison Harvard accepts 4.6% of its college applicants. [154]

Why Combinator?

The Y Combinator Accelerator boasts one of the best track records with a portfolio valued at more than $300 billion,[155] and more than 30 unicorns (startups with valuations over $1 billion dollars) graduated from their program.[156] Some of the most prominent graduates are Airbnb, Door Dash, Stripe, Cruise, Instacart, Drop Box, Coinbase, and Zapier. Y Combinator's success is a combination of the fellow members in the cohorts, the mentor network, and the alumni network, which resembles a fraternity of the most successful startups. These cohorts, mentors and alumni help each other with introductions to customers, investors, and strategic resources. They become each other's first customers, creating a self-sustaining growth engine. As Dave McClure of 500 Startups famously said, "YC is a VC fund that looks and operates like a guild of geeks, and hardly looks anything like a traditional fund composed of VC partners with MBAs or finance degrees. They are operators, through and through."[157]

Y Combinator's philosophy is simply stated, "We think founders are most productive when they can spend most of their time building. Our goal is to create an environment where you can focus exclusively on building product and talking to users."[158]

Upon indoctrination into Y Combinator, founder Paul Graham welcomes everyone by saying:

> "You're one of us. You are now part of Y Combinator. There's nothing that you can do or say or screw up so badly that we'll change our minds. If something dramatically bad happens, come to us first that's why we're here. We're there for you when things go down. And believe us. No matter how catastrophic things seem to you, we've seen this before. There's no way we're going to turn our backs on you. You're now part of the family."

This purposeful message gives entrepreneurs the freedom to stop trying to impress each other and eliminates the wasted energy on hiding flaws and failures.

Jessica Livingston, spouse of founder Paul Graham and a partner at YC, highlights a few things to do to not fail; make something people really want, stay focused, measure your growth, and keep your expenses low. So, cracking the secret formula of accelerator success may have been best concluded on the timing of launching Y Combinator in 2005. As it rode the wave of the best entrepreneurs relocating to Silicon Valley to launch their businesses, Y Combinator brought together the right people, at the right time, in the right place. Then, their early success of a few participants led to higher expectations. The tides rose as unicorns after unicorns executed against really big goals. They created a concentrated way to focus startups on exponential theory.

Much like many other accelerators, Y Combinator hosts weekly conferences on raising capital, design thinking, and growth hacking. Y Combinator focuses on making sure the founders become efficient in raising capital as it is 50% of the job of the founder in a high growth accelerator startup. Design thinking is learning to frame, ideate, and generate creative solutions by modeling, prototyping, drawing, sketching, analyzing, and testing products or services. Growth hacking is rapidly testing ideas against the customer journey, scaling ideas that grow the company and iterate on ideas that do not. Y Combinator also host dinners that draw the likes of Mark Zuckerberg and Marc Andreessen, who build a circle of trust by sharing unfiltered stories not for public consumption. This continued to develop big thinkers. As shared on Y Combinator website, "the general atmosphere is like a modernist version of an Oxford college dining hall, but without a high table."[159] The lore of these dinners builds upon the secret societies, high expectations, and creates the inner sanctum of the Silicon Valley greats.

Y Combinator also does many of the same things other accelerators do for budding entrepreneurs and innovators, like hosting office hours, demo days, and provide the best contacts for fundraising. They even partnered with crowdfunding startup WeFunder, a YC graduate, to let investors like you and me participate. They also offer prototype days, rehearsal days, alumni demo days, and alumni speaking engagements. They even created an online startup school open to everyone interested, enrolling over 20,000 founders in each session. This happened by accident, when a glitch in the Y Combinator startup school acceptance email admitted all 15,000 people who applied to their 3,000-seat course. However, they decided to make that the new norm and now accepts everyone.[160] Y Combinator is a model worth noting as they have likely been at the center of the global value creation engine over the last 15 years. They live exponential theory.

Other top accelerators, such as 500 Startups, also started in Silicon Valley, have democratized innovation by helping companies from over 75 countries and have materialized eight unicorns[161]. TechStars, started in Boulder, Colorado, has a global portfolio in over 60 countries and nine unicorns.[162] Other networks like GAN, the Global Accelerator Network, which spans the globe with over 120 accelerators and startup studios, offer a network of corporate partners, perks, and education for leading startups through these short-term rapid accelerations.[163] The rapid growth of accelerators throughout the world is moving the center of the digital tidal wave away from Silicon Valley into startup communities around the world such as New York, Boston, Los Angeles, Austin, London, Paris, Tel Aviv, Singapore, and Shanghai.

An accelerator's ability to efficiently test ideas allows it to provide a startup with a better chance to succeed. Time spent on the wrong solution wastes valuable resources and can easily kill a startup. The goal, then, is to fail fast, often, early, and cheaply, in order to rapidly learn, iterate, grow, and scale. This optimized equation has presented a problem for companies not thinking about their future in this way and leaves behind those that can't make decisions fast enough. Accelerators aren't just investing in a business model, but in a combination of a problem worth solving, a management team, a network, and lean, iterative and agile execution. Accelerators test ideas in a scientific, evidence-based way to determine if they're worth investing in further. Once proven, these ideas get the follow-on investment needed to grow exponentially. This data-driven approach is one of the reasons why accelerators have helped fundamentally change how leaders solve future problems and measure future success.

The growth mindset makes no problem too big to solve. The growth mindset is the ability to solve problems, faster through continuously learning, adapting, and continuous incremental improvements every day that led to exponential growth. A great example of the growth mindset is the video created by the Door Dash founders for their application to Y Combinator. They were looking to create software to help small business owners, so they went and talked to hundreds of potential customers and realized that small restaurants in Palo Alto couldn't afford to deliver food even though their customers wanted it. They also found a sizable number of delivery drivers who were seeking a side hustle. So, they created PaloAltoDelivery.com and with minimal marketing they got 150 customers in just their first month.[164] Their focus on finding a problem worth solving, and then learning, adapting, and continuously improving every day led them to a successful proto- type, an acceptance to Y Combinator, and eventually, a multi-bil- lion-dollar IPO (Initial Public Offering).

With the rise in crowdfunding and crowdsourcing, compa- nies are also investing in innovation prizes like the X Prize, Hero X, PnG's Innocentive platform that crowdsources ideas, or many foundations like Gates, Rockefeller and others putting out prizes to move entire industries forward. This creative way to advance an idea for the greater good is being used more and more. Elon Musk recently announced an investment of over $100 million dollars X Prize to carbon capture to reverse the harmful effects of pollu- tion. The four-year prize will give 15 groups $1 million, and 25 $200,000 scholarships to students, while first prize will take $50 million, second $20 million and third prize $10 million. "The goal of this competition is to inspire entrepreneurs and engineers to build the carbon dioxide removal solutions, many of which have only been discussed and debated," X Prize founder and executive chairman Peter Diamandis shared.[165] "We want to see them built, tested, and validated," he added. "We hope this X Prize will acti- vate the public and private sectors to get involved in the same way that the $10 million Ansari X Prize brought about the commercial spaceflight industry." This is likely to set off innovation and raise billions of dollars to compete for the prize.

Measuring Success

The way that we measure a business's success will need to change. Companies are already focused on the triple bottom line as the masses demand more from companies than ever before. Triple bottom line focuses on social, environmental, and financial success. Leaders need to find metrics that share progress in each of these areas. No longer can companies focus just on profit. Impact funds have proven that this is a winning formula for companies and investors alike.

Beyond new metrics, leaders must also become futurist. Leveraging foresight, leaders will harness data to understand new relationships between information, creating knowledge from the patterns that emerge, and new insights from the connectedness of disparate systems. This will require leaders to pivot their purpose and business model to stay in front of the disruption all around them. Leaders will need to identify the preferred future and rally the troops around the needed actions to pivot. The inability to make decisions will likely create an undesirable future leaving a company to the graveyard of companies' past.

Leaders need to frame the future around shifting to new business models aligned with metrics that create focus on its purpose. The future will demand leaders continually scan signals, forecast, and iterate on strategies that bring the company's purpose and ecosystem together around a common vision. Leaders will need to stress that their business models be repeatable, predictable, scalable, and sustainable, all while being adaptable, sustainable, and equitable as they seek their companies to survive and hopefully become exponential.

- Repeatable
- Predictable
- Scalable
- Sustainable

What gets measured gets done. So, shifting focus to measuring success in new ways will be important to companies' ability to accelerate innovation and thrive in a world that will require them to make decisions at light speed. Understanding how to create a compelling disruptive company in a short time and staying out of the negative news cycle are both vital.

The future belongs to the companies investing in ideas and innovation able to outgrow the corporate behemoths, disrupting themselves. These companies can leverage the same process and strategies that Y Combinator built their success on. Yet, the future will also require these businesses to also choose purpose over profit. As we recognize during the great reset of COVID-19, companies will need to start to make decisions and create innovation that is fast to market and good for the world. Exponential theory is the solution.

REFLECTION

We are our habits. Innovation Labs and Accelerators help startups and companies develop with the best habits to be successful.

- How did your company find the problem/solution fit?
- What was your MVP?
- How do you collect customer feedback? How do you iterate?
- What is the product/market focus for your company?
- What processes are repeatable?
- What in your business is predictable?
- How can you scale your growth?
- How can you make your company more sustainable?

Chapter 12.

The Great Reset

"Our deepest fear is not that we are inadequate.
Our deepest fear is that we are powerful beyond measure."
—Marianne Williamson

A New Beginning

As the Earth took a deep breath in 2020, we got a glimpse into the much-needed reset. The environment glaringly showed the benefit of a reset during the COVID-19 pandemic. Small changes in human habits, such as orders to work from home, drastically improved many parts of biodiversity. In March 2020, after only four days of quarantine, Los Angeles recorded the best air quality in 40 years.[166]

At the same time, China pollution dropped by up to 30% depending on the region and India up to 70%, resulting in smog disappearing from the cities for the first time in decades. Soon after the shutdown in India, towns that had not seen the Himalaya in 30 years had a new skyline with the mountains suddenly appearing from over 200 kilometers away.[167] The empty beaches in Florida offered turtles record years for offspring.[168] The world got to take a breather and nearly every inhabitant benefited. The glimpse into the great reset has provided us with data and images that we cannot ignore, and we must begin to take action. The power of thinking big and exponential theory has never been more needed.

Nature has shown signs of great resilience to reverse much of the damage caused by unsustainable decisions. Chernobyl, the deadliest nuclear power meltdown in history, caused humans to abandon the city over 35 years ago. Now, since humans left the city, nature has taken back over. Through a process called radiosynthesis, even radiotrophic fungi have been discovered absorbing radiation and converting it into harmless chemical energy.[169] This is the resilience of this wonderful planet.

Chernobyl is an example we don't want to see in the rest of the world, although it clearly shows humans are violently disrupting the natural systems. With this environmental trauma, Earth is not in danger, humans are in danger. The solutions are simple if the behavior of the masses starts to recognize the needed change. We need a new approach; to think circularly, sustainably, and humanely in everything we do. This is a reasonable request for the greater good of the people and the planet.

We must consider better strategies to transition to clean energy as we will otherwise create many unintended consequences. For example, moving from carbon energy to clean energy too quickly will disrupt our own current energy demands. Nonetheless, we must take action. Cost is only one of the variables to consider, along with the skills of the current workforce, and worker's compensation needed to move from one industry to another. When we think big, we can address the many other issues from trying to make a simplified change. The need for empathy for all sides become very important for the success of any change initiative. The over hundred-year-old electrical grid is one of America's greatest achievements, enabling a homeowner to have electricity hundreds of miles away from the power plant. Yet, with the increased demands from the electrification of nearly everything, the system is reaching a breaking point.

This is further exacerbated by the pressure to use renewables, such as solar and wind. These sources only perform at competent levels when the sun is shining on them or the wind is blowing. The need for storing energy locally could be the promise of harnessing the sun to handle peak hour demand near the end of the day. Also, technologies such as energy efficient light bulbs, energy efficient appliances, load balancing by controlling digital thermostats like Nest, during peak time, and increased battery power provide hope for a more sustainable future. Although, the immediate needs are likely to go unmet as the public has put too much pressure on price, moving to renewables, all while not wanting to lose consumption. This pressure is not only impacting the decisions we make on the environment, but also human rights.

The great reset also was the rebirth of a much-needed civil rights movement. After a three-month lockdown, George Floyd was murdered after he was knelt on for 9:24. He gasped for breath and over 70% of America watched the video in horror. The outpouring and empathy led to the largest civil right demonstrations in history.

We've already seen more vocal groups of people step up to lead conversations about police brutality, #metoo, voting access, healthcare, refugee crises, LGBTQ rights, diversity and inclusion, income inequity, gun violence, food insecurity, hate crimes, safe spaces, and criminal justice reform. These issues have put equality on center stage in the desperate need of a reset.

In the United States, slavery may be considered America's "original sin," not solved by our founding fathers in the US Constitution nor America's deadliest military conflict, the Civil War. From the Civil War sprouted the passage and ratification of the 13th, 14th, and 15th amendments, all on the surface appearing good, yet allowed systemic racism to fester. The promise of these amendments was further eroded by Jim Crow, state, and federal laws; all of which were decisions made by groups that did not represent the people it impacted. We must think bigger.

However, we have been slow to address these problems, both of equality and of environmentalism. This lack of progress has caused the wounds to grow deeper and more severe. Moreover, those affected are caught in chronic trauma. The chronic trauma paralyzes us, and nobody can move forward. Much like the brain in *Thinking Fast and Slow*; creativity and innovation are impossible when we're stuck between fight, flight, or freeze.

The 24/7 news cycle has also inflicted trauma. While stuck at home, we've been drudged through a daily assault of negative news. The mental health impact of isolation and negativity is a recipe for disaster. Thinking big is how we can lift ourselves out of this cycle of trauma, but it comes with the caveat that progress takes time; even exponential growth has its own deceptive phase.

Since progress is not an overnight absolute, but rather a complex, methodical, and laborious process, we must view progress on a spectrum. Humans like to think they are absolute creatures with right and wrong and black and white, but we're re-learning to view ourselves on spectrums, with shades of grey. We all live on a variety of spectrums in different areas of our lives. We have spectrums of sexuality, mental health, empathy, leadership, and more. Viewing both ourselves and progress on spectrums allows us to be more fluid and less rigid. When we are more fluid, we can be more understanding, empathetic, and adaptable.

While these wicked problems have gotten so bad and the situation seems so dire, we must agree to solve the problems but be realistic about it how to take action. Change will not happen overnight without drastic unintended consequences. After all, most of this book was about how change was too fast for most and disruption swept industries away. We will need the biggest change makers in our world-big thinkers and exponential organizations-to lean into these issues to make the world a better place for all people. Accelerated change is what we have left to rely on, and it must bring about change for our people, and for our planet, and for the purpose of any company. The fantastic part about it is that if there is dynamic, powerful change for humans and the environment, companies will grow more than ever before-and their profits will grow with them. All in the name of saving the world.

Purpose over Profit

In January 2020, Larry Fink, the founder and CEO of the world's largest asset manager BlackRock wrote an open letter to global CEOs about the future of finance. Fink stated that BlackRock would make investment decisions based on sustainability. He announced that it would begin to exit from investments in companies that had negative sustainable outcomes, like coal. At the time, BlackRock had over $7 trillion in assets, so this was a big deal. Boldly, Fink claimed, "we are on the edge of a fundamental reshaping of finance."[170] It is no hyperbole to say that with this letter, Fink shook the corporate world.

BlackRock's commitment to investing with a focus on Environmental, Societal, and Governmental (ESG) investment factors was one of the first major commitments for big businesses to become conscious businesses. Leaders of the future like Fink are realizing that ESG investments aren't just a good thing to do, they're a great investment opportunity. As the problems of the world will impact us all, investments in companies that solve problems of such a universal importance are more likely to grow exponentially. ESG has grown to encompass $35 trillion of the $90 trillion global economy.[171]

Fink's critics argued that backing the ESG movement was just a marketing campaign. They argued that BlackRock's statement was intended to further insulate it from suspicion and investigation. Then, two months later, COVID-19 shut the world down and caused a global shift as nearly every industry experienced a great reset. ESG investments, meanwhile increased, led by Tesla's major value growth, as well as a doubling of sustainability-oriented mutual funds.[172]

After the protest of the summer of 2020, BlackRock also put out a call to action to CEOs asking them to release the racial, ethnic, and gender makeup of their workforce and boards, stating "we are raising our expectations,"[173] warning that they will vote against leaders who don't act. It is blasphemous that there are currently only four Black CEOs in the Fortune 500,[174] because if the diversity was truly representative of the population, there would be almost 65 Black CEOs on the list. Adhering to the ESG criteria will force leaders of the future to reset how they view business and the implications of the decisions on the world. In Larry Fink's 2021 annual letter, he doubled down on his previous commitment to sustainability, calling all companies to "disclose a plan for how their business model will be compatible with a net-zero economy."[175]

Now, a measure of a company's success is not only about profit and loss, but also about quantifying the impact the company is making both socially and environmentally. People, planet, and profit, the triple bottom line, is how we will measure companies and innovation moving into the future. Larry Fink highlights that "companies with better ESG profiles are performing better than their peers, enjoying a 'sustainability premium.'"[176] BlackRock has proven that doing the right thing is good for profit. BlackRock is embracing exponential theory.

Social media and video technology has enabled us to witness and expose different atrocities that cannot be ignored. Mass connectivity has increased global accountability, and consumers are not letting leaders skirt responsibility for their actions. The Great Reset will demand a mindset shift for organizations to survive the oncoming pressures of the skeptical masses.

A Conscious Movement

To accomplish this mindset shift, companies are embracing a holistic approach to innovation. This will drive growth through impact and more purposeful business models. We see a rise of impact-driven investing, B-Corp, Conscious Capitalism, circular and purpose-driven business. This is welcomed as it protects capitalism, which has come into question as systemic issues continue to increase awareness on issues that need to be solved. Conscious capitalism drives leaders to do the right thing as capitalism continues to raise the tides for humans as we are in the process of ushering in a massive shift from scarcity to abundance.

As major companies pivot to join BlackRock in its commitment to ESG, there's a new wave of social innovation. Goldman Sachs subsequently committed to investing over $750 billion in climate mitigation, adaptation, and risk management.[177][178]

Microsoft's commitment to be net carbon-negative will eliminate the carbon footprint it has accrued since 1975, while also launching an initiative to teach 25 million people the digital skills needed as a result of the COVID transition to working from home.[179][180]

Google has been carbon neutral since 2007, and they strive to be carbon free by 2030.[181] Meanwhile, it has committed $175M to racial equality.[182] Apple has also committed to be 100% carbon neutral by 2030,[183] and additionally to build out a Racial Equity and Justice Initiative, creating an education hub for Historical Black Colleges and Universities and an Apple Developer Academy in Detroit, Michigan.[184]

Facebook aims to be carbon neutral supported entirely by renewable energy sources by 2030 too.[185] Facebook also commits $200 million to Black owned businesses and $10 million to groups, "working on racial justice."[186]

Tesla started creating a baseline summary of their emissions use to formulate its future environmental goals and is also tracking how many tons of carbon dioxide Tesla cars have saved.[187188] Tesla created a Diversity, Equity, and Inclusion team to implement its diversity strategy.[189]

Lastly, Amazon created The Climate Pledge, promising to become carbon neutral by 2040, ten years ahead of the Paris Climate Agreement's goal of 2050. Steps it has taken so far include purchasing 100,000 electric vehicles for delivery[190], and buying the new Seattle NHL Arena and naming it Climate Pledge Arena to bring awareness to the importance of companies committing to impact the future.[191]

Leaders need to start to embrace feedback, listen carefully to customers, and continue to improve their product or service based on the voice of the customers, all customers. All while executing on their purpose, treating everyone fairly, and taking care of the environment. Seems reasonable. The new generation of customers is fed up with greed, unfair employment practices, environmental damage, and companies that are not responsible to do the right thing. Social media is starting to create accountability. So, companies need to think bigger.

Companies must consider how to be better corporate citizens and make a social impact, while competing for customers. A conscious organization will be the only organization that survives. As exponential leaders raise consciousness, the world heads toward a circular economy that removes waste, promotes environmental healing, zero impact, and a societal shift toward access, equality, and accountability. With new information technologies and useful data, companies will have to take action for the whole instead of the parts. Transparency and openness will require companies to be conscious and responsible to all stakeholders in the future.

Big thinking leaders recognize that it's simply best for businesses to design a better world. Healing the planet is now the responsibility of everyone and big businesses are starting to take the lead as social media, whistleblowers, and the media put everything under the microscope. Companies are incentivized to create solutions to eliminate poverty for billions of people, improve global health, and create a more diverse workforce that represents the communities they serve. Leading by example is no longer optional.

The reason Gates, Page, Brin, Zuckerberg, Jobs, Bezos, and Musk have earned so much money is that they have added and captured great value by providing services that many customers would now have a hard time living without. Some may argue that the widening gap between the super-rich and the rest of the world is regressive. However, en route to making these stockpiles of money, each first had to solve a problem that created value for their customers.

We will also likely see most of this money given away in the next couple of generations, as Bill Gates and Warren Buffett created the Giving Pledge. The Giving Pledge encourages the world's billionaires to give more than half of their wealth away. Over 200 billionaire philanthropists have signed up for the Giving Pledge, and according to Wealth-X, it could be worth over $600 billion by 2022.[192] This major influx of philanthropy will create entirely new industries in social equity, climate, and health like we've never seen before.

Elon Musk may be on target to become the first trillionaire on our planet, but instead of counting his money, consider the change he has already created in energy, space, AI, and every other industry to which he sets his mind. Musk will likely do incredibly good things for both the planet and humans via sustainable energy, self-driving cars, and space exploration. Further, when leaders stop demonetizing, democratizing, and dematerializing the world, their companies will likely stop growing. Leaders are not immune to disruption. Jeff Bezos even predicts that "Amazon is not too big to fail . . . In fact, I predict one day Amazon will fail. Amazon will go bankrupt. If you look at large companies, their lifespans tend to be thirty-plus years, not a hundred-plus years."[193]

With data, AI, and machine learning, we will soon be able to predict problems before they even actualize. As exponential technologies become less deceptive and more commonplace, there will be more data available to analyze than ever before, making all technology infinitely more powerful. Computing power will soon pass the power of the human brain and in less than one generation computing power will pass the power of all human brains.[194]

Technology continues to challenge humanity's norms in light of new information. Now, meat is being recreated in a laboratory from plant proteins, just as nearly every other food has been recreated before it. With hydroponics and vertical farming, we have an opportunity to reimagine the food chain and improve life for every living being in the food chain. Companies such as Foodini have created 3D printed food. In the future, delivery may even be instant as you will be able to download a Michelin 5-Star Chef recipe from halfway around the world and print dinner. We will likely print clothes from 3D printers and reuse the materials for the next day outfit. We are even starting to print 3D houses solving some of the world's most basic problems.

Massively transformative solutions to food, clothing and shelter are only the beginning of the process of providing the world with abundance. We are quickly shifting from business models based on scarcity to models of abundance that change how we will look at everything. Yet, technology is in a purgatory, with many positive advancements, and we need to start assessing its impact on other parts of our lives. All of these ExOs face involuntary side effects from the impact of their technology. Only time will tell which companies will survive the onslaught of new leaders leveraging the ten ways of thinking big.

The Ten Ways of Thinking Big

Much like how exponential technologies compound upon each other and become increasingly faster and more powerful, exponential theory must compound the ten ways of thinking big to reimagine the future.

Here are the Ten Ways of Thinking Big:

1. Embracing the VUCA world

Accelerating change and disruption have created a volatile world that has forced us to shift how we solve wickedly complex problems. While solving these complex problems, leaders of the future must constantly seek vision, understanding, clarity, and agility. To achieve this, future leaders will also need a guiding massive transformative purpose, continuous team communication, empathy, and active listening. They must place an emphasis on diversity and data to simplify, create expectations, and educate as we seek to experiment, fail, learn, and repeat.

2. Thinking Exponentially

The combination of mass access and exponential technologies has enabled exponential growth. Bill Gates and Microsoft made computers useful, and in turn, became the first exponential organization. Leaders of the future will need to incorporate elements of ExOs into their businesses (IDEAS & SCALE), leverage the

6Ds of Disruption, and follow the laws of exponential growth. How could you apply exponential thinking to your company?

3. Digitizing the Model

Through digitization, companies can dematerialize, demonetize, and democratize their industry and disrupt the competition. Just ask Blockbuster, Kodak, or journalists how that feels. To even exist in the future, a company must digitize as much as they can, and shift to a world of abundance and away from scarcity. Digitizing the model is a requirement. What can you start to digitize in your company?

4. Becoming a Tech Company

Companies need to shift towards becoming tech companies, like Domino's and Starbucks. These companies invested in becoming a tech company to win the pizza and coffee wars respectively. New companies can start tech-first, like Uber and Airbnb, to provide people with access over ownership. Moving forward, how can we create our own ecosystems with our businesses? What technology platform can we use to deliver value to customers efficiently over and over again?

5. Finding the Massive Transformative Purpose

Exponential growth is so ridiculously fast that we need massive transformative purposes to stay focused. Google set out to organize the world's information, and when it outgrew that purpose, it created Alphabet. Leaders must set their teams up for success-and scalability by creating massively transformative goals. What is your massive transformative purpose?

6. Launching Disruption

Apple continues to push the cutting edge of personal technology from iPod to iPhone to Apple Watch. Each time they launch a new product, they wield disruption to many other industries. Viewing product launches from the eyes of a major disruptor better frames the size and scope each product must bring, before it becomes obsolete. What is your iPhone moment?

7. Leveraging the Viral Loop

The viral loop of Facebook, Instagram, and WhatsApp continues to provide a platform to connect with relevant people, ideas, companies, and movements. Facebook, of course, serves as its own platform for social change, now possibly more powerful than the media and government messaging combined. Leaders of the future must be wary of the viral loop, both in its potential for major growth, but also that of major failure. Everything leaders do in the future can go viral, instantly, and thinking before acting has never become more important. How can our companies leverage the viral loop?

8. Playing the Long Game

Amazon grew from an online bookseller to one of the biggest companies on Earth with inventiveness and patience. The focus on sustainability and the long term will be essential for survival. When strategically mapping out their own business, leaders should sacrifice short term returns for major long-term gains. Further, their goals should not only satisfy an MTP, but also a goal that provides the company adequate longevity, like Bezos' vision in 1997 to make Amazon Earth's most customer-centric company. How can we focus our companies on a longer-term vision?

9. Executing the MVP

Elon Musk continues to achieve impossible goals like creating the fastest electric car or the reusable rocket, and it starts with a vision and a "Minimum Viable Product" prototype. Soon, clean energy will demonetize and democratize while healing the planet. Of course, Musk is also readying himself for Plan B—colonizing Mars if all else fails. Elon has shown the world that no idea is too crazy, as long as there is a focus on solving the right problem. How can we make our first product so the world can see our vision?

10. Accelerating Innovation

Accelerators are a breeding ground for major disruptors. Companies continue to create innovation labs. All businesses must seek to become repeatable, predictable, scalable, and sustainable. Leaders must acknowledge that unless what they're doing can be easily tested and validated, it's going to fail. How can we accelerate innovation to move from ideation to launch in as little as twelve weeks?

With exponential theory, it becomes possible to reimagine everything. The solutions to the wicked problems that plague our people, planet, and profits are at our fingertips.

Saving Our World

With the world in chaos, we see more and more people leaning in and stepping up to humanity than stepping away. Change is the only certainty, and a seismic shift has occurred that is unlikely to slow down. The momentum calls leaders to action, using exponential theory to solve our greatest global challenges.

One thing is certain, we are all going to die one day. Until that day, we can choose to play big or small. Every day is a choice to step into the exponential, venture into the unknown, understand the world, reinvent our potential, and expand our own self-limiting box. As our circle of concern grows, our impact on the world will too. The key to a really successful business is for leaders to find a problem they're passionate about, create a solution, and think as big as possible on how it can impact the world. We are in need for more leaders like these to step into the future.

In the next twenty years, with exponential theory, leaders of the future will be able to create business models that address all the United Nations' (UN) Sustainable Development Goals.[195] The UN identified the global goals as a blueprint for a better and more sustainable world for every person on the planet. All these goals are achievable if we think big and leverage exponential theory to reimagine the future:

Reimagine poverty,

Reimagine hunger,

Reimagine health,

Reimagine education,

Reimagine gender equality,

Reimagine clean water and sanitation,

Reimagine renewable energy,

Reimagine work and economic growth,

Reimagine infrastructure,

Reimagine inequalities,

Reimagine sustainable cities and communities,

Reimagine responsible consumption,

Reimagine climate action,

Reimagine life below water,

Reimagine life on land,

Reimagine justice,

Reimagine peace . . .

The future doesn't lie in our governments saving the day and taking care of the people. The future belongs to entrepreneurs, innovators, visionaries, and anyone who can reimagine their world and disrupt themselves in the process. The future belongs to us. Over the next 20 years, join us in thinking big and the power of the exponential theory to reimagine our future.

Let's get started!

REFLECTION

We are all one. The Great Reset showed us more than ever how interlaced all of us are. This Great Reset calls on each of us to lean into change and do the right thing even when nobody is looking for the good of us all.

- What can you do differently to impact your world?
- What can you do professionally to make a difference every day?
- How can you move your company to think bigger?
- How can you share this message to be part of the solution?

Learn more about Exponential Theory

Exponential Theory is more than a book, it is a movement being created by a set of entrepreneurs, innovators, and leaders who want to impact the world, who want to leave a legacy, and who want to build something significantly bigger than themselves. Thinking exponential is the start point. Are you able to see how you could impact 1 billion people?

If you want to be this kind of leader in the future, it is important for you to join a group that will support each other to obtain these types of goals. At Exponential Theory we've worked with over 500 organizations and have over 20+ years' experience assisting in the creation of some of the most innovative companies in the world. Join us to further understand exponential theory, practice it, and master the ability to take a strategy, people, and technology to solve some of the world's biggest problems. Learn more how you can become proficient implementing all that you've learned in this book personally, professionally, and organizationally.

Visit http://www.exponentialtheory.com to learn more about our courses, workshops, podcast, consulting, facilitating, and coaching. Enjoy the journey!

Glossary of Key Terms and Concepts

Exponential *Theory* calls on leaders to become complex adaptive problem solvers, and to accomplish this, we have included a variety of mental models, mindsets, and frameworks in this book. This glossary defines key terms and concepts *as they relate to the exponential theory* and may be a different usage than typical definitions.

1984: The infamous 1984 Apple Super Bowl commercial that promoted the personal computer, Macintosh, as a play on George Orwell's famous book with the same title.

500 Startups: The Accelerator with eight Unicorns in over 75 Countries.

Abundance: Through disruption, scarcity is out and abundance is in. How can you make your idea available to everyone?

Accelerators: A process to fast-track startups with problem/solution fit, customer feedback, product/market fit, scaling, mentoring, fundraising, and a relentless focus on innovation.

Accelerating Change: Exponential leaders understand that change is speeding up.

Access Over Ownership: The idea that for a small fee, users can access something without the need to purchase it. The fundamental of a sharing economy.

Agility: The ability for a lean organization to quickly pivot, make mistakes, and iterate to avoid disruption and capitalize on successes.

Algorithms: Leverage data, math, and systems to solve problems.

Allen, Paul: Co-founder of Microsoft.

Alexa: The Amazon voice-AI that is the epitome of customer service. Alexa continues to learn skills and improve integration with the rest of Amazon's exponential technologies, and now has many devices—integrated into the TV, car, convenience store, pharmacy, mobile phone, and at every point of sale.

Amazon Web Services: a system that Amazon built internally to power its own service but the pay-as-you-go cloud platform that fully integrates business applications for developers, companies, and governments alike.

Apple's Pirate Ship: Apple's Innovation Lab.

Artificial Intelligence: The ability for computers to make decisions and process information. See list of exponential technologies.

Augmented reality: Technology that enabled a layer of images and computers on top of the real world. See list of exponential technologies.

Automation: Technologies that perform automatically, found in the smart home, smart city and leveraging cloud, data, AI and machine learning. See list of exponential technologies.

Autonomy: Self-organizing, multidisciplinary teams operating with decentralized authority.

Autonomous Vehicles: Technology that enabled level 5 autonomous driving, allowing users to ride, not drive. See list of exponential technologies.

B-Corp: Businesses that meet the highest standards of verified social and environmental performance, public transparency, and legal accountability to balance profit and purpose.

Bitcoin: an open-source killer-app to eliminate the middleman, let users be the bank, while serving the unbanked and underbanked, built atop the blockchain.

Bogle, John: Founder of Vanguard that outlined the company in his senior thesis at Princeton.

Bezos, Jeff: Founder of Amazon, trades places as richest man in the world. The master of the long game.

Benz, Karl: Inventor of the combustion engine.

Bell, Alexander Graham: Inventor of the telephone.

Blockchain: The interconnected system of third-party ledger verification that cryptocurrency is built on. An exponential technology for FinTech.

Carbon Neutral: Balancing Carbon Dioxide emissions with removing the same amount that are created.

Community and Crowd: If you build communities and you do things in public, you don't have to find the right people—they find you.

Conscious Capitalism: States that while profits are essential for a vital and sustainable business, conscious capitalism focuses on purpose beyond the profit

Customer Centricity: Continuous feedback on MVP, new solutions, and new business models will make it inexpensive to improve the performance: build, collect feedback, iterate, and repeat.

Dashboards: A real-time, adaptable dashboard with all essential company and employee metrics, accessible to everyone in the organization.

Data: Exponential leaders will measure everything as data will become the new currency. As former CEO Jack Welch of General Electric (GE) shared, "What you measure gets done," and exponential leaders get it done. Another phrase: Data is the new oil.

Diamandis, Peter: Co-Creator of the 6D's of disruption, founder of the X-Prize Foundation, and Co-Founder of Singularity University.

Donald Keck's Law of Fiber: states that fiber optic cables double in power every nine months, twice as fast as computing power.

6Ds: Once something is digitized, it becomes exponential.

The 6Ds are Digitization, Deception, Disruption, Dematerialization, Demonetization, and Democratization. In succession, these principles explain exponential growth.

Digitization: Process of bringing things online that were previously offline.

Deception: When the exponential curve is below linear line and where the perceived value is low despite of gaining momentum.

Disruption: The moment where exponential growth overtakes linear growth.

Dematerialization: When technology shrinks into smaller technologies or disappears.

Demonetization: Technology causes the price of products and services to decrease.

Democratization: When technology becomes available to everyone, everywhere.

ESG Investments: A commitment to investing with a focus on Environmental, Societal, and Governmental (ESG) factors.

ExOs—Exponential Organizations: All have massive transformative purposes and have four or more of both internal and external attributes. Internal attributes can be remembered as IDEAS; Interfaces, Dashboards, Experimentation, Autonomy, and Social Technologies. External attributes can be remembered as SCALE; Staff on Demand, Community & Crowd, Algorithms, Leveraged Assets, and Engagement.

Exponential Leader: Future leaders will have vision, understanding, clarity, and agility to focus on their long-term innovations.

Exponential Mindset: Rather than thinking in terms of incremental growth, the ultra-successful aim for "hockey stick" growth—or increasingly bigger achievements at a faster rate.

Fink, Larry: Founder and CEO of the World's largest asset manager BlackRock. Writes a transformative open letter to CEO's each year.

FOMO: Stands for the Fear Of Missing Out, a principle that subconsciously forces users to compete with one another on social media.

Foresight: The ability to understand new relationships between information, create knowledge from emerging patterns, and gain new insights from the connectedness of disparate systems.

Gale-Shapley Algorithm: Also known as the stable marriage algorithm, this algorithm matched people with one another and won the Noble Prize in 1962.

Gates, Bill: Co-founder of Microsoft that claimed he would "put a computer on every desk in every home." Now Gates is a mega philanthropist that was advocating for a Pandemic response plan years before COVID-19.

Growth Mindset: Knowledge is power, and education is the one thing no one can take away from you. The more you learn, the more you realize what you don't know.

Great Reset: A call for global unity out of the devastating impacts of the COVID-19 crisis, avoid going back to the same pre-COVID world.

Hardwired Brain: Synapse are 90% formed by age 5, creating automatic responses to nearly everything we deal with in life.

Hyperloop: Air powered prototype train that would travel up to 760mph.

Interfaces: ExOs have very customized processes for how they interface with customers and other organizations.

Jobs, Steve: The founder of Apple, who had impeccable timing that guided Apple to releasing the iPod, iPhone, and iPad each with their own growing successes.

Kahneman, Daniel: Author of Thinking Fast & Slow, proved the brain has two systems. System One is fast, conscious, effortless, and automatic. System Two is slow, deliberate, conscious, effortful, and controlled.

Kotler, Steven: Author and co-creator of the 6D's of disruption.

Leveraged Assets: Holding onto what's critical and outsourcing everything else. Access not ownership.

Mass Access: The democratization of access, over 5-billion smart phones and growing.

Massive Transformative Purpose: The guiding principle for an ExO that has such an incredibly broad statement that will impact at least a billion people.

Moonshots: Companies will need to continuously innovate, focusing on creating new solutions that are moonshots, loonshots, or mars shots to disrupt business as usual. Creating a safe place to do this will be the future for every company.

Moore's Law: Law that computing power doubles every eighteen months.

Musk, Elon: The founder of Tesla and SpaceX, Musk is an expert at creating a Minimum Viable Product to launch even the wildest of ideas.

Newmark, Craig: Founder of Craigslist that inadvertently demonetized newspaper ad revenue and contributed to the decline of news objectivity.

NFT: Non-fungible tokens are unique and unreplaceable digital stamps, creating scarcity in abundance.

PageRank: The original algorithm by Larry Page at Google that sorted content users were looking for and became the basis of Google's search engine today.

Page, Larry: Google Founder and father of PageRank.

Platform: If the market doesn't exist for an exponential idea, build your own market, like Uber, Airbnb, Craigslist, or Amazon.

Pocket Crystal: The iPhone before there were iPhones, complete with messaging and emoticons. "If there were a fire in my house I'd think family first, pocket crystal second."—Marc Porat.

Porat, Marc: The man who first coined the term the "information economy," he also created what was essentially the iPhone, the Pocket Crystal, but it was only 1990 and it was too early for users to want the Pocket Crystal.

Ray Kurzweil's Law of Accelerating Returns: states that technology will leverage other technologies and constantly and automatically improve itself. Thus, technological progress is exponential.

Reimagine: To reinterpret imaginatively; rethink.

Repeatable, Predictable, Scalable, Sustainable: Business models of the future must be all of these things, or else they will fail.

Robert Metcalfe's Law: states that networking power is squared with each user that joins a network, automatically creating exponential potential from the start.

SaaS: Software as a Service is a new business model that sells software instead of a traditional service/product.

Sasson, Steve: Kodak employee that invented the digital camera.

Scientific Method: The proven way to test hypothesis and how entrepreneurs prove assumptions.

Sculley, John: The marketing executive that led Pepsi and then led Apple, ultimately leading to Steve Job's departure from Apple.

Sharing Economy: Future business models will leverage the sharing, gig, and subscription economies to optimize access and democratize their products and services.

Showrooming: The concept where users look at a product in store, but then buy it online anyways. Amazon popularized this as they hammered traditional shopping malls and department stores.

Skunk Works: The Lockheed Martin Innovation Lab that built a fighter jet in 143 days.

Smith, Fred: Founder of FedEx that first paper outlining it got a C in college.

Social Technologies: Social technologies, or collaborative technologies, allow organizations to manage real-time communication among all employees.

Staff on Demand: Minimize full-time staff and outsource tasks. Uber uses staff on demand when they incentivize drivers to go online during busy times.

Tech Companies: In the future, only tech companies will survive.

Ten Thousand Hours: Ten thousand hours of deliberate practice is needed to become an expert in your field.

Ten Thousand Experiments: Iteration on the Ten Thousand Hours rule by Michael Simmons, "Deliberate experimentation is more important than deliberate practice in a rapidly changing world."

Thinking Big: Considering all of the complexities of a situation, balanced with patience and a massive transformative purpose.

TRIZ: The Theory of Inventive Problem Solving by Genrich Altshuller found 1,500 basic problems and 40 universal answers to solve them all.

Triple Bottom Line: Companies must now be responsible for three outcomes: societal, environmental, and financial.

Two-Pizza Teams: Intimate groups of builders within Amazon that can be fed by no more than two-pizzas. They're empowered with the freedom to invent, experiment, and wait.

Unicorn: A startup with a billion-dollar valuation.

UN Sustainable Development Goals: The global goals as a blueprint for a better and more sustainable world for every person on the planet.

Viral Content: With the law of networks and mass connectivity, the time to share an idea, product, or solution with the world becomes instantaneous. All companies in the future will be tech companies and content companies.

Viral Loop: A self-sustained mechanism that drives continuous referrals for continuous growth.

VUCA (Old): Describes a circumstance that is Volatile, Uncertain, Complex, and Ambiguous

VUCA (New): A model for leaders to exist in the VUCA world; Vision, Understanding, Clarity, Agility

We're the Product: The idea that users exchange their data in order to use a product or service for free; because the data the businesses harness from the user is what they're actually seeking.

X Prize: The organization that supports innovation competitions started by Peter Diamandis. Most notably a $100M prize with Elon Musk for Carbon Capture.

Yahoo: The former internet juggernaut and largest company in the world that failed to innovate and ended up sold for 5% of their peak value.

Y-Combinator: The Accelerator with over 30 Unicorns in its alumni portfolio.

List of Exponential Technologies

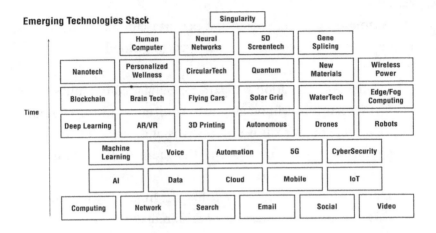

			Singularity		
	Human Computer	Neural Networks	5D Screentech	Gene Splicing	
Nanotech	Personalized Wellness	CircularTech	Quantum	New Materials	Wireless Power
Blockchain	Brain Tech	Flying Cars	Solar Grid	WaterTech	Edge/Fog Computing
Deep Learning	AR/VR	3D Printing	Autonomous	Drones	Robots
Machine Learning	Voice	Automation	5G	CyberSecurity	
AI	Data	Cloud	Mobile	IoT	
Computing	Network	Search	Email	Social	Video

Emerging Technologies Stack (Time ↑)

Artificial Intelligence-the ability for computers to make decisions and process information.

Data-although data is not new, it is new currency of the new economy.

Cloud-storing data in the cloud has enabled us to untangle ourselves from the office, access over ownership.

Mobile-as we walk around with our iPhone or Android phones, we enable massive amounts of solutions to serve us from our pocket.

Internet of Things (IoT) – sensors and devices collecting and sharing data.

Machine Learning-ability for machines to learn and interact with systems.

Voice Recognition-technology that interacts with voice commands, Amazon's Alexa was the first mass solution that leveraged data, AI and machine learning to continue to improve the interaction.

Automation-technologies that perform automatically, found in the smart home, smart city and leveraging cloud, data, AI and machine learning.

5G-the 5th generation standard for cellular communications.

Cybersecurity-technologies to secure our current computing environment, with privacy concerns and quantum computing approaching in the near future. This industry will continue to drive change for companies.

Deep Learning-is AI that acts like the human brain, processing data and creating patterns for decision making.

Augmented reality-technology that enabled a layer of images and computers on top of the real world.

Virtual reality-technology that alters the landscape, taking users into a new reality.

3D Printing-ability to print 3-dimensional material products, soon to be printing cars, food, homes and clothing.

Autonomous Vehicles-technology that enabled level-5 autonomous driving, allowing users to ride, not drive.

Drones-technology that begin as a hobby industry, yet with AI, data, maps, robotics and other applications, drones provide another layer of logistics and delivery.

Robotics-technologies leveraging automation, AI, data, machine learning, and mechanical output, possibly in autonomous cars, drones or assembly.

Blockchain-a ledger of records, completely transparent and open for everyone to see every transaction.

Brain Tech-neurotechnology's are learning how to balance the brain, leveraging neuroplasticity with many optimal effects.

Flying Cars-as soon as cars go autonomous, they will also take to the air and get us from A to B even faster.

Solar-the ability for solar to create things off the grid, cars can leverage solar, and homes can too.

Water Tech-technologies that are producing water from thin air using decompression and then desalination technologies creating usable water from the ocean.

Edge Computing-technologies that bring computing power to distributed networks enabling other technologies to better leverage the cloud.

Nanotech-micro technologies that will miniaturize just about everything enabling personalized wellness to robust solutions on the internet of things.

Food Tech-alternative meats, 3D-printed food, and vertical hydroponic gardens will create a more sustainable ecosystem and lessen the burden and strain on population growth, while improving the health of everyone.

Personalized Wellness-the ability for us to create personalized plans based on DNA, microbiome, blood type, and millions of other data points.

Circular Tech-technologies enabling the sustainability of products full life-cycle taking into account manufacturing to disposal, cradle to grave for every resource we use.

Quantum Computing-the ability for computer to process qubits instead of bits and bytes, creating exponential processing power.

Space Tech-companies like SpaceX are privately delivering Astronauts to the International Space Station and soon transporting people from Shanghai to New York in 40 minutes, and even potentially mining Asteroids for trillions of dollars of precious resources.

Wireless Power-the ability to charge things from a distance, no more power issues for anything. A shift to abundance.

Computer-Brain Interface-the ability for a computer to communicate with the brain enabling technologies to be controlled by the mind alone.

Neural Networks-the ability for computers to think like a human.

5D Tech-the ability for humans to interface with computers through brain-computer interfaces, smelling, touching and experiencing through a full sensory experience.

Gene Splicing-the ability to rewrite DNA by splicing genes and introducing Stem Cells.

Singularity-A hypothetical moment in time when artificial intelligence and other technologies have become so advanced that humanity undergoes a dramatic and irreversible change.

About the Authors

Aaron D. Bare

Aaron Bare is a strategist, entrepreneur, and author. He has also held leadership roles in strategy, innovation, technology, marketing, and sales. He is a results-focused exponential leader who understands how to create a high-performing culture. Aaron has been a lecturer on innovation and entrepreneurship for over  ten years. As a global facilitator, he traveled to over ninety countries and all fifty states. He holds an MBA from Thunderbird School of Global Management, an MA from Indiana University, and a BSc (with Honors) from Indiana Institute of Technology. He lives in Arizona.

N. Forbes Shannon

Forbes Shannon is an entrepreneur, writer, musician, and comedian. He graduated from Barrett, the Honors College at Arizona State University with a non-profit management degree as both a writing fellow and entrepreneurship and innovation fellow. An avid investor in his community, Forbes strives to help his networks  solve problems with high energy and optimism. Forbes served as a member of the leadership team that puts on the largest annual entrepreneurship convention in Arizona, Phoenix Startup Week. He lives in Arizona.

Endnotes

Chapter One

1   Arizona PBS, "Early Childhood Brain Development has Lifelong Impact," 2017, https://azpbs.org/2017/11/early-childhood-brain-development-lifelong-impact/#:~:text=90%20Percent%20of%20a%20Child's%20Brain%20Develops%20by%20Age%205

2   National Centers for Environmental Information, "Link Between Earth's Heat and Hurricane's Strength Grows," (May 19, 2020) https://www.ncei.noaa.gov/news/link-between-heat-and-hurricanes

3   Insurance Information Institute, "Facts + Statistics: Tornadoes and Thunderstorms," (2021) https://www.iii.org/fact-statistic/facts-statistics-tornadoes-and-thunderstorms

4   International Tsunami Information Center "Frequently Asked Questions," (2021) http://itic.ioc-unesco.org/index.php?option=com_content&view=article&id=1133&Itemid=2155

5   Thomas Friedman, "Global Weirding is here," *New York Times* (February 17, 2010) https://www.nytimes.com/2010/02/17/opinion/17friedman.html

6   World Wildlife Foundation "WWF's Living Planet Report reveals two-thirds decline in wildlife populations on average since 1970," wwf.panda.org, (September 9, 2020) https://wwf.panda.org/wwf_news/?793831/WWF-LPR--reveals-two-thirds-decline-in-wildlife-populations-on-average-since-1970

7   World Health Organization, "Zoonoses: Emerging Zoonoses," (2021) https://www.who.int/zoonoses/emerging_zoonoses/en/

8   "*The Need to Grow*" directed by Rosario Dawson (2018) Film. https://grow.foodrevolution.org

9   P.J. Crutzen "Geology of mankind" *Nature* Vol 415, p. 23-23 (2002) https://www.nature.com/articles/415023a

10   Achenbach, Joel, "British Forces Burned the US Capitol in 1814," *The Washington Post* (January 6, 2021) https://www.washingtonpost.com/history/2021/01/06/british-burned-capitol-1814/

11   Jon Kolker, *"Wicked Problems: Problems Worth Solving."* (Austin Center for Design, 2012)

12   Christine Peterson, "25 Years After Returning to Yellowstone, Wolves Have Helped Stabilize the Ecosystem." *National Geographic*, (July 10, 2020) https://www.nationalgeographic.com/animals/2020/07/yellowstone-wolves-reintroduction-helped-stabilize-ecosystem

13   *"Seaspiracy"* directed by Ali Tabrizi. Film. (2021) NetFlix

14   "What is the Seventh Generation Principle?" *Indigenous Corporate Training*. Accessed August 1, 2020. https://www.ictinc.ca/blog/seventh-generation-principle

15   Rebecca Harrington, "This Incredible Fact Should Get You Psyched About Solar Power," *Business Insider* (September 29, 2015) https://www.businessinsider.com/this-is-the-potential-of-solar-power-2015-9

16   Entreprneur.com, "Fred Smith: An Overnight Success," (October 9th, 2008) https://www.entrepreneur.com/article/197542

17   Veronika Kero, "Investor Jack Bogle Founded his Legendary Company Based on his Princeton Senior Thesis," *CNBC.com*, (January 17, 2019) https://www.cnbc.com/2019/01/17/investor-jack-bogle-founded-company-based-on-princeton-senior-thesis.html

18   "Our Impact" Plastic Bank. Accessed July 1, 2020. https://plasticbank.com/our-impact/

19   "Meet the Technology" Zero Mass Water. Accessed July 1, 2020. https://www.zeromasswater.com/rexi/

20   Patagonia, "Buy Less, Demand More," Accessed April 5, 2021. https://www.patagonia.com/buy-less-demand-more/

21   Hannah Denham, "Pandora Ditching Mined Diamonds for Lab-Gown Ones," *The Washington Post*, (May 4, 2021)https://www.washingtonpost.com/business/2021/05/04/pandora-diamond-lab-mining/

22   "Our Mission" Tony's Chocolonely. Accessed July 1, 2020. https://tonyschocolonely.com/us/en/our-mission

23   Scott Reyburn, "JPG File Sells for $69 Million, as 'NFT Mania' Gathers Pace," *New York Times*, (March 11, 2021) https://www.nytimes.com/2021/03/11/arts/design/nft-auction-christies-beeple.html

Chapter Two

24   Noor Ahmad Khalidi, "Afghanistan: Demographic Consequences of War 1978-1987" *Central Asian Survey*, Vol. 10, No. 3, (1991): 101-126

25   Bob Johansen, *"Leaders Make the Future: Ten New Leadership Skills for an Uncertain World"* (Berrett-Koehler Publishers, 2012)

26   Terrence Szymanski, "Papyrus Making 101: Rediscovering the Craft of Making Ancient Paper," *University of Michigan Library System* (2004)

27   "Manchester to Liverpool: The First Inter-City Railway," *BBC Manchester* (July 23rd, 2009)

28   "Benz Patent Motor Car: The First Automobile," Diamler, accessed June 28th, 2020 https://www.daimler.com/company/tradition/company-history/1885-1886.html

29   Elon Musk, *"Hyperloop Alpha"* (Tesla.com, 2013), 6, https://www.tesla.com/sites/default/files/blog_images/hyperloop-alpha.pdf

30   Marina Koren, "What Would Flying From New York to Shanghai in 39 Minutes Feel Like?" *The Atlantic*. October 3rd, 2017. https://www.theatlantic.com/technology/archive/2017/10/spaccx-elon-musk-mars-moon-falcon/541566/

31   Daniel Kahneman, *Thinking Fast and Slow*, (Farrar, Straus & Giroux: New York, 2011)

32   History.com Editors "Automated Teller Machines" *A&E Television Networks*, April 20, 2010, https://www.history.com/topics/inventions/automated-teller-machines

Chapter Three

33   Hannah Bae, "Bill Gates's 40th anniversary email: 'Goal was a computer on every desk,'" CNN Money, April 6, 2015, https://money.cnn.com/2015/04/05/technology/bill-gates-email-microsoft-40-anniversary/

34   Microsoft News Center, "Microsoft Acquires Skype for $8.5 Billion," Microsoft News, May 10, 2011, https://news.microsoft.com/announcement/microsoft-acquires-skype/

35   Microsoft News Center, "Microsoft to Acquire LinkedIn," Microsoft News, June 13, 2016, https://news.microsoft.com/2016/06/13/microsoft-to-acquire-linkedin/

36   Microsoft News Center, ""Microsoft to Acquire GitHub for $7.5 Billion," Microsoft News, June 4th, 2018, https://news.microsoft.com/2018/06/04/microsoft-to-acquire-github-for-7-5-billion/

37   Salim Ismail et al., *Exponential Organizations: Why new organizations are ten times better, faster, and cheaper than yours (and what to do about it)* (New York: Diversion Books, 2014)

38   Ismail, *Exponential Organizations...*

39   Jeff Bezos, *2020 Letter to Shareholders*, SEC.gov, 2020

40   'How Long Does it Take to Reach 50 Millions Users" VisualCapitalist, last modified June 8th, 2018.

41   Direk Desmet et al., *"Six Building Blocks for Creating a High Performance Digital Enterprise"* McKinsey & Company (September 2015)

42   "Moore's Law," *Wikipedia,* https://en.wikipedia.org/wiki/Moore's_law

43   Jeff Hect, "Is Keck's Law Coming to an End?" *ieee.org,* January 26, 2016 https://spectrum.ieee.org/semiconductors/optoelectronics/is-kecks-law-coming-to-an-end

44   "Metcalfe's Law," *Wikipedia*, https://en.wikipedia.org/wiki/Metcalfe%27s_law

45   Ray Kurzweil, "The Law of Accelerating Returns" *Kurzweillai.net* (March 1, 2001)

46   Chris Morris. "GameStop is Finally Cashing in on the Reddit Stock Frenzy," *Fortune.* (April 5, 2021) https://fortune.com/2021/04/05/gamestop-stock-gme-sale-ryan-cohen-wallstreetbets-reddit-chewy-founder/

47   John Mackey & Raj Sisodia, *Conscious Capitalism,* (Brighton, Harvard Business Review Press, 2012)

48   "Exponential Primer," Singularity University, July 1, 2020, https://

su.org/concepts/

49   Mike Saviage, Colleen Rodriguez, "Adobe Surpasses $11 Billion in Annual Revenue," Adobe, December 12, 2019 https://www.adobe.com/content/dam/cc/en/investor-relations/pdfs/21219102/aN8ujHV4loX5.pdf

50   Patrick Seitz, "Adobe CEO Touts 'Textbook Transition' to the Cloud," investors.com, December 30, 2016 https://www.investors.com/news/technology/adobe-systems-ceo-touts-textbook-transition-to-cloud/

51   Peter Diamandis, "The 6 D's," diamandis.com https://www.diamandis.com/blog/the-6

52   Peter Diamandis, Steve Kotler, *Bold: How to Go Big, Create Wealth, and Impact the World* (New York: Simon & Schuster, 2016)

53   Made in Space. Accessed August 1, 2020. https://madeinspace.us/about/#timeline

54   Jack Nicas, Keith Collins, "How Apple's Apps Topped Rivals in the App Store it Controls," New York Times, September 9, 2019 https://www.nytimes.com/interactive/2019/09/09/technology/apple-app-store-competition.html#:~:text=More%20than%20two%20million%20apps%20are%20available%20on%20the%20App%20Store.

55   Alex Osterwalder, Yves Pigneur, et al., *The Invincible Company*, (Strategyzer, April 14, 2020)

Chapter Four

56   Walgreens ramps up Redbox Rollout. May 8, 2008. CSP Daily News. https://www.cspdailynews.com/technologyservices/walgreens-ramps-redbox-rollout

57   Tiffany Hsu, "The World's Last Blockbuster Has No Plans to Close." *New York Times*. (March 6, 2019) https://www.nytimes.com/2019/03/06/business/last-blockbuster-store.html

58   Edmund Lee, "Everyone You Know Just Signed Up for Netflix," *New York Times*, April 21, 2020 https://www.nytimes.com/2020/04/21/business/media/Netflix-q1-2020-earnings-nflx.html

59   Gregory Ferenstein, "Read What Facebook's Sandberg Calls Maybe 'The Most Important Document Ever to Come Out of the Valley."

TechCrunch. (January 13, 2013) https://techcrunch.com/2013/01/31/read-what-facebooks-sandberg-calls-maybe-the-most-important-document-ever-to-come-out-of-the-valley/

60   Dana Mattioli "Their Kodak Moments," *Wall Street Journal*, January 6, 2012, https://www.wsj.com/articles/SB10001424052970203513604577142701222383634#:~:text=At%20its%20peak%2C%20Eastman%20Kodak,work%20for%20the%20imaging%20pioneer.

61   Looking back at 35 years of the digital camera, MacWorld, January 4, 2011. https://www.macworld.com/article/1156514/35yearsofdigitalcameras.html

62   Marguerite Reardon, "Why Cisco Killed the Flip Mini Camcorder," *CNET*, April 13, 2011, https://www.cnet.com/news/why-cisco-killed-the-flip-mini-camcorder/

63   Arjun Kharpal, "Microsoft Unveils $25 Nokia Phone in Low-End Push," *CNBC*, August 11, 2014, https://www.cnbc.com/2014/08/11/microsoft-unveils-25-nokia-phone-in-low-end-push.html#:~:text=Microsoft%20has%20released%20a%2019,the%20fast%2Dgrowing%20emerging%20markets.

64   Angel Au-Yeung, "Why Billionaire Craig from Craigslist is Giving Millions to Journalism and Education," *Forbes*, August 13, 2018, https://www.forbes.com/sites/angelauyeung/2018/08/13/why-billionaire-craig-of-craigslist-is-giving-millions-to-journalism-and-education/#5333f47f7942

65   Gavin Butler. "Bitcoin Mining Could Use More Energy Than All of Italy by 2024" *Vice News*.(April 7, 2021) https://www.vice.com/en/article/dy8amw/bitcoin-mining-energy-consumption

Chapter Five

66   James F. Peltz, "Domino's Pizza Stock is Up 5000% Since 2008, Here's Why," *Los Angeles Times*, May 15, 2017, https://www.latimes.com/business/la-fi-agenda-dominos-20170515-story.html

67   Yoni Blumberg, "Domino's Stock Outperformed Apple and Am-

azon Over the Last Seven Years-Now it's the World's Largest Pizza Chain," CNBC, May 1, 2018 https://www.cnbc.com/2018/03/01/no-point-1-pizza-chain-dominos-outperformed-amazon-google-and-apple-stocks.html

68   "Dominos 101: Fun Facts," Domino's, Accessed July 1, 2020 https://biz.dominos.com/web/public/about-dominos/fun-facts

69   Conor Grant, "Starbucks Borrows Billions From its Own Customers....with Gift Cards," *The Hustle*, August 27, 2019 https://thehustle.co/starbucks-gift-cards-financing-borrowing/

70   Number of Starbucks Locations Worldwide 2003-2020, Finance Online. https://financesonline.com/number-of-starbucks-worldwide/

71   HR & A Advisors "Economic Impacts of AirBnB," October 22, 2013, https://www.airbnb.com/press/news/new-study-airbnb-generated-632-million-in-economic-activity-in-new-york

72   Rani Molla, "AirBnB is On Track to Rack Up More Than 100 Million Stays This Year," *VOX,* July 19, 2017, https://www.vox.com/2017/7/19/15949782/airbnb-100-million-stays-2017-threat-business-hotel-industry

73   "AirBnB Community Tops $1.15 Billion in Economic Activity in New York," AirBnB, May 12, 2015 https://www.airbnb.com/press/news/airbnb-community-tops-1-15-billion-in-economic-activity-in-new-york-city

74   "AirBnB Fast Facts," AirBnB, July 1, 2020 https://news.airbnb.com/fast-facts/

75   "Our Story," Marriott International, July 1, 2020, https://www.marriott.com/about/culture-and-values/history.mi#ourstory

76   "AirBnB Fast Facts," AirBnB

77   Theodore Schleifer, "AirBnB Sold Stock at a $35B Valuation, but What is it Really Worth?" *VOX* March 19, 2019, https://www.vox.com/2019/3/19/18272274/airbnb-valuation-common-stock-hoteltonight

78   "Our Story," Marriott International, July 1, 2020, https://www.marriott.com/about/culture-and-values/history.mi#ourstory

79   "Uber Elevate," Uber, July 1, 2020, https://www.uber.com/us/en/elevate/

80   Bernhard Friedrich, "The Effect of Autonomous Vehicles on Traffic," *Autonomous Driving*, (May, 2016) https://link.springer.com/chapter/10.1007/978-3-662-48847-8_16

81   "Road Traffic Injuries & Deaths: A Global Problem," *Center for Disease Control*, December 18, 2019, https://www.cdc.gov/injury/features/global-road-safety/index.html

Chapter Six

82   "Usage Share of Web Browsers," *Wikipedia,* July 1, 2020, https://en.wikipedia.org/wiki/Usage_share_of_web_browsers#cite_note-17

83   "US Leading Streaming Video Platforms by Monthly Users," Statista, July 1, 2020, https://www.statista.com/statistics/910875/us-most-popular-video-streaming-services-by-monthly-average-users/#:~:text=Leading%20U.S.%20video%20streaming%20services%202019%2C%20by%20monthly%20average%20users&text=The%20most%20popular%20video%20streaming,with%20just%20under%2026.5%20million.

84   Dan Noyes, "Top 20 Valuable Facebook Statistics," *Zephoria*, June 2020 https://zephoria.com/top-15-valuable-facebook-statistics/

85   Myles Udland, "Check Out Yahoo's Market Cap Over Time," Business Insider, July 25, 2016, https://www.businessinsider.com/yahoo-market-cap-over-time-2016-7

86   Salim Ismail, "Massive Transformative Purpose-The Heartbeat of Every ExO," Medium, June 11, 2018, https://medium.com/@salimismail/massive-transformative-purpose-the-heartbeat-of-every-exo-8f59e7a811b4

87   Larry Kim, "Why Google's Larry Page Only Buys Companies that Pass His Crazy Toothbrush Test," *Inc.com*, August 28, 2014, https://www.inc.com/larry-kim/how-google-s-ceo-only-buys-companies-that-pass-his-crazy-toothbrush-test.html

88   Meg Prater, "25 Google Search Statistics to Bookmark ASAP," HubSpot Blog, February 18, 2020, https://blog.hubspot.com/marketing/google-search-statistics

89   Daniel Strauss, "Here's Why One Analyst Thinks YouTube is

Worth $300 Billion," *Markets Insider,* October 29, 2019, https://markets. businessinsider.com/news/stocks/youtube-value-as-separate-company-is-300-billion-analyst-says-2019-10-1028641059

90   Dan Tynan, "The History of Yahoo and How it Went From Phenom to Has-Been," *Fast Company,* March 21st, 2018, https://www.fastcompany.com/40544277/the-glory-that-was-yahoo

91   Tynan, "The History of Yahoo…"

92   Prater, "25 Google Search Statistics to Bookmark ASAP"

93   "The Prize in Economic Sciences 2012," Nobel Prize, October 15, 2012, https://www.nobelprize.org/prizes/economic-sciences/2012/press-release/

94   Kyle Loung, Dr. Gregory Pavlov, "Matching Theory: Kidney Allocation," *University of Western Ontario Medical Journal,* 2016, http://www. uwomj.com/wp-content/uploads/2013/10/v82no1_6.pdf

95   Kate Conger, "Google Removes 'Don't be Evil,' Clause for its Code of Conduct," *Gizmodo,* May 18, 2018, https://gizmodo.com/google-removes-nearly-all-mentions-of-dont-be-evil-from-1826153393

96   Wikipedia, "Usage Share of Web Browsers" (2021) https:// en.wikipedia.org/wiki/Usage_share_of_web_browsers

97   Inc. Magazine, "How Google's 20% rule can make you more energetic and productive." https://www.inc.com/bryan-adams/12-ways-to-encourage-more-free-thinking-and-innovation-into-any-business.html

98   "Smartphone Market Share," IDC, June 22nd, 2020, https:// www.idc.com/promo/smartphone-market-share/os

99   Lily Hay Newman, "Google Will Delete Your Data by Default-in 18 Months," *Wired Magazine,* June 24, 2020, https://www.wired.com/story/google-auto-delete-data/

100   Zoe Chance et al., "How Google Optimized Healthy Office Snacks," *Harvard Business Review,* March 3rd, 2016, https://hbr. org/2016/03/how-google-uses-behavioral-economics-to-make-its-employees-healthier

101   Charles Duhigg, "What Google Learned From its Quest to Build the Perfect Team," *New York Times,* February 25th, 2016, https://www.

nytimes.com/2016/02/28/magazine/what-google-learned-from-its-quest-to-build-the-perfect-team.html

102   "G is for Google," Larry Page, *Alphabet*, July 1, 2020, https://abc.xyz/

103   Michael Schneider, "Google Gets 2 Million Applications a Year," Inc.com, July 26, 2017, https://www.inc.com/michael-schneider/its-harder-to-get-into-google-than-harvard.html

Chapter Seven

104   "Marc Porat," Computer History Museum, July 1, 2020, https://computerhistory.org/profile/marc-porat/#:~:text=Marc's%20PhD%20dissertation%2C%20The%20Information,there%20U.S.%20economy%20and%20workforce.

105   "Information Technology," Merriam-Webster, July 1, 2020, https://www.merriam-webster.com/dictionary/information%20technology

106   CHM,"Marc Porat"

107   Bhaskar Chakravorti et al., "Which Countries are Leading the Data Economy," *Harvard Business Review*, January 24, 2019, https://hbr.org/2019/01/which-countries-are-leading-the-data-economy

108   Sarah Kerruish dir et al., "General Magic," (2018: New York, Spellbound Productions II) documentary/film

109   Kerruish, "General Magic"

110   Kerruish, "General Magic"

111   "Apple Alumni: Where are They Now?" Forbes.com, July 1, 2020, https://www.forbes.com/pictures/fdee45ehjd/john-sculley/#3216a70c1534

112   Michael Malone, *Infinite Loop: How Apple, the World's Most Insanely Great Computer Company, Went Insane,* (New York: Currency/Double-Day, 1999)

113   "1984 (advertisement)," Wikipedia, July 1, 2020, https://en.wikipedia.org/wiki/1984_(advertisement)

114   "John Sculley," Wikipedia, July 1, 2020, https://en.wikipedia.org/wiki/John_Sculley

115   "U.S. Recorded Music Revenues by Format," *RIAA,* July 1, 2020, https://www.riaa.com/u-s-sales-database/

116   Angela Monaghan, "Nokia: The Rise and Fall of a Mobile Phone Giant," *The Guardian*, September 3, 2013, https://www.theguardian.com/technology/2013/sep/03/nokia-rise-fall-mobile-phone-giant

117   Brian Merchant, *The One Device: The Secret History of the iPhone* (London: Transworld, 2017)

118   Roberta Naas, "Apple Watches Outsell the Entire Swiss Watch Industry, but Don't Ring the Death Bell Yet," *Forbes*, February 7th, 2020, https://www.forbes.com/sites/robertanaas/2020/02/07/apple-watch-es-outsell-entire-swiss-watch-industry-but-dont-ring-the-death-bell-ye-t/#2ed7a63978f1

119   Dan Reisinger, "Apple's AirPods Business is Bigger Than You Think," *Fortune*, August 6th, 2019, https://fortune.com/2019/08/06/ap-ple-airpods-business/

Chapter Eight

120   Dan Noyes, "Top 20 Valuable Facebook Statistics," *Zephoria*, June 2020 https://zephoria.com/top-15-valuable-facebook-statistics/

121   Douglas Clark, Corinne Wier, "eMarketer Reduces US Time Estimates for Facebook and Snapchat," *eMarketer*, May 28, 2019, https://www.emarketer.com/newsroom/index.php/emarketer-reduces-us-time-spent-esti-mates-for-facebook-and-snapchat/

122   J. Clement, "Facebook Users Reach by Device," *Statista*, May 18, 2020, https://www.statista.com/statistics/377808/distribution-of-face-book-users-by-device/

123   "Instagram Marketing," Facebook for Business, July 1, 2020, https://www.facebook.com/business/marketing/instagram

124   David Kushner, "The Flight of the Birdman: Flappy Bird Creator Dong Nguyen Speaks Out," *Rolling Stone*, May 11, 2014, https://www.rollingstone.com/culture/culture-news/the-flight-of-the-birdman-flappy-bird-creator-dong-nguyen-speaks-out-112457/

Chapter Nine

125   "Our DNA," Amazon Jobs, July 1, 2020, https://www.amazon.jobs/en/working/working-amazon/#our-dna

126   Nathan Bomey, "Borders' Expansion Hastened it's Implosion," *The Ann Arbor News,* July 19, 2011, http://www.annarbor.com/business-review/borders-rapid-rise-accelerated-its-fall/

127   "Borders Group Inc. Annual Report 2007," Securities Exchange Commission, February 3, 2007, http://media.corporate-ir.net/media_files/irol/65/65380/site/includes/pdfs/10k.pdf

128   John Biggs, "There is One New Book on Amazon Every Five Minutes," *Telecrunch,* August 21, 2014, https://techcrunch.com/2014/08/21/there-is-one-new-book-on-amazon-every-five-minutes/#:~:text=In%20an%20interesting%20post%2C%20writer,were%20added%20in%20a%20day.

129   Arie Shpanya, "Loss Leading in an eCommerce World," *Wiser,* February 25, 2014, https://blog.wiser.com/loss-leading-ecommerce-world/

130   Marianne Wilson, "The Most Profitable Retailers in Sales Per Square Foot Are..." *Chain Store Age*, July 31, 2017, https://chainstoreage.com/news/most-profitable-retailers-sales-square-foot-are#:~:text=The%20No.,of%20%243%2C721%20per%20square%20foot.

131   Jeff Bezos, "Amazon 1997 Shareholder Letter," *SEC.gov,* 1997, https://www.sec.gov/Archives/edgar/data/1018724/000119312513151836/d511111dex991.htm

132   Tae Kim, "Walgreens, CVS and Rite-Aid lose $11 Billion in Value After Amazon Buys Online Pharmacy PillPack," *CNBC,* June 28th, 2018, https://www.cnbc.com/2018/06/28/walgreens-cvs-shares-tank-after-amazon-buys-online-pharmacy-pillpack.html

133   Paul Farhi, "Jeffrey Bezos, Washington Post's Next Owner, Aims for a New 'Golden Era' at the Newspaper," Washington Post, September 3rd, 2013, https://www.washingtonpost.com/lifestyle/style/jeffrey-bezos-washington-posts-next-owner-aims-for-a-new-golden-era-at-the-newspaper/2013/09/02/30c00b60-13f6-11e3-b182-1b3bb2eb474c_story.html

134   "Amazon 2016 Letter to Shareholders," SEC.gov, 2016, https://www.sec.gov/Archives/edgar/data/1018724/000119312517120198/d373368dex991.htm

135   Malcolm Gladwell, *Outliers*, (New York: Little, Brown and Com-

pany, 2008)

136   Michael Simmons, "Forget the 10,000 Hours Rule; Edison, Bezos, and Zuckerberg Follow the 10,000-Experiment Rule," *Medium*, October 26, 2017, https://medium.com/accelerated-intelligence/forget-about-the-10-000-hour-rule-7b7a39343523#:~:text=The%20idea%20is%20that%20you,class%20performer%20in%20any%20field.

137   "Incremental Growth in Cloud Spending Hits a New High While Amazon and Microsoft Maintain a Clear Lead," *Synergy Research Group*, February 4th, 2020, https://www.srgresearch.com/articles/incremental-growth-cloud-spending-hits-new-high-while-amazon-and-microsoft-maintain-clear-lead-reno-nv-february-4-2020

Chapter Ten

138   Alyssa Pagano, Irene Anna Kim, "How Tesla CEO Elon Musk Makes and Spends his $19.2 Billion," *Business Insider*, June 24th, 2019, https://www.businessinsider.com/tesla-elon-musk-ceo-net-worth-makes-spends-billion-money-2019-6

139   "Elon Musk Quotes," Goodreads.com, July 1, 2020, https://www.goodreads.com/quotes/6526560-my-proceeds-from-the-paypal-acquisition-were-180-million-i

140   "About Tesla," Tesla.com, 2020, https://www.tesla.com/about

141   Danielle Muoio, "Karma Revero Has Solar Roof," *Business Insider*, August 11, 2016, https://www.businessinsider.com/karma-revero-has-solar-roof-photos-2016-8

142   Musk, "Master Plan."

143   Musk, "Master Plan."

144   Ash Maurya, *Scaling Lean: Mastering the Key Metrics for Startup Growth*, (London: Penguin Press Limited, 2016)

145   Maurya, *Scaling Lean*.

146   "Tesla Overtakes Toyota to Become World's Most Valuable Carmaker," BBC, July 1, 2020, https://www.bbc.com/news/business-53257933#:~:text=Tesla%20overtakes%20Toyota%20to%20become%20world's%20most%20valuable%20carmaker,-1%20July%20

2020&text=Tesla%20has%20become%20the%20world's,stock%20
hit%20a%20record%20high.

147   Associated Press, "Elon Musk Tweets About Mysterious Tunnel
Project," *Wall Street Journal*, January 26, 2017, https://www.wsj.com/arti-
cles/elon-musk-tweets-about-mysterious-tunnel-project-1485407280

148   Koren, "Shanghai,"

149   Musk, "Hyperloop."

150   "Missions: Mars," SpaceX, July 1, 2020, https://www.spacex.com/
human-spaceflight/mars/

151   Ryan Morrison, James Pero, "Elon Musk's SpaceX Will Launch a
NASA Mission to an Asteroid," DailyMail, March 4th, 2020
https://www.dailymail.co.uk/sciencetech/article-8074995/Elon-Musks-
SpaceX-launch-NASA-mission-metal-rich-asteroid.html

Chapter Eleven

152   Don Reisinger, "Why Apple is Flying a Pirate Flag Over its HQ,"
Fortune, April 1, 2016, https://fortune.com/2016/04/01/apple-pirate-flag/

153   Brian Dunbar, "Your Device Has More Power," *Nasa.gov* (September 12th, 2013) https://www.nasa.gov/mission_pages/voyager/multimedia/
vgrmemory.html#.YFtKCi1h1pQ

154   Foti Panagiotakopoulos, "How to Get Into Y Combinator According to the Founders that Did Get In," GrowthMentor.com (March 16, 2021)
https://www.growthmentor.com/blog/how-to-get-into-y-combinator/

155   Y Combinator. "YC Top Companies" (January 2021) https://
www.ycombinator.com/topcompanies

156   CrunchBase. "Y Combinator Portfolio Unicorns" (2021) https://
www.crunchbase.com/lists/y-combinator-portfolio-unicorns/b536478c-
314d-44d6-ac48-220067cecc21/organization.companies

157   Drew Hansen, "What's the Secret Behind Y Combaintor's
Success?" *Forbes.com* (February 18, 2013) https://www.forbes.com/
sites/drewhansen/2013/02/18/whats-the-source-of-y-combinators-suc-
cess/?sh=292254327e70

158   Y Combinator "About Y Combinator" (April 2020) https://www.

ycombinator.com/about/#:~:text=We%20think%20founders%20are%20 most,product%20and%20talking%20to%20users.

159   Y Combinator. "What Happens at Y Combinator," (2016) https:// www.ycombinator.com/atyc/

160   Theodore Schleifer "Y Combinator Accidentally let 15,000 People Into an Exclusive Program-and Now Has Decided to Do It On Purpose," *Vox.com* (February 27, 2019) https://www.vox. com/2019/2/27/18241034/y-combinator-startup-school-expansion

161   500 Startups, "Protfolio," (2021) https://500.co/startups

162   Techstars, "Techstars Companies," (2021) https://www.techstars. com/portfolio

163   GAN, "2021 Data Report" (2021) https://www.gan.co/ data/2021-accelerator-data-infographic/

164   Y Combinator "DoorDash's Application Video for YC S13" (December 9, 2020) https://www.youtube.com/watch?v=Rzlr2tNSl0U

165   Mike Wall, "Elon Musk, X Prize Unveil $100 Million Carbon-Capture Contest," *Space.com* (February 9th, 2021) https://www.space. com/elon-musk-carbon-capture-x-prize

Chapter Twelve

166   Tony Barboza, "L.A. Coronavirus Clean Air Streak Has Already Come to an End. Here's Why." *LATimes* (April 28, 2020) https://www. latimes.com/environment/story/2020-04-28/coronavirus-la-air-quality-improved-pandemic-dont-expect-it-to-last

167   [ii] Soutik Biswas, "India Coronavirus: Can the COVID-19 Lockdown Spark a Clean Air Movement?" *BBC* (April 21 2020) https://www. bbc.com/news/world-asia-india-52313972

168   Richard Luscombe, "Florida: Endangered Sea Turtles Thriving Thanks to COVID Restrictions," *The Guardian,* (April 19, 2020) https:// www.theguardian.com/us-news/2020/apr/19/florida-leatherback-turtles-coronavirus-beaches

169   Bob Yirka, "Testing Chernobyl Fungi as a Radiation Shield for Astronauts," *phys.org,* (July 27, 2020) https://phys.org/news/2020-07-cher-

nobyl-fungi-shield-astronauts.html

170   Andrew Ross Sorkin, "BlackRock CEO Larry Fink: Climate Crisis Will Reshape Finance," *New York Times*, (February 24, 2020) https://www.nytimes.com/2020/01/14/business/dealbook/larry-fink-blackrock-climate-change.html

171   Alex Diaz, "Time for ESG Companies to Lead On Adaptation," *Medium*, April 13, 2020, https://medium.com/predict/time-for-adaptation-esg-eca866e113

172   Aaron Ross Sorkin, BlackRock's Chief Pushes a Big New Climate Goal for the Corporate World," *New York Times* (January 26th, 2021) https://www.nytimes.com/2021/01/26/business/dealbook/larry-fink-letter-blackrock-climate.html#:~:text=Fink%20wrote%20a%20letter%20to,a%20fundamental%20reshaping%20of%20finance.%E2%80%9D

173   Saijel Kishan, "BlackRock to Push Companies on Racial Diversity in 2021," Bloomberg, (December 9th, 2020) https://www.bloomberg.com/news/articles/2020-12-10/blackrock-plans-to-push-companies-on-racial-diversity-in-2021

174   Phil Wahba, "Only 19: The Lack of Black CEOs in the History of the Fortune 500," *Fortune,* (February 1, 2021) https://fortune.com/longform/fortune-500-black-ceos-business-history/#:~:text=That%20will%20leave%20only%20four,Ren%C3%A9%20Jones%20at%20M%26T%20Bank.

175   Sorkin, "BlackRock's Larry Fink..."

176   Larry Fink, "Larry Fink's 2021 Letter to CEOs," *BlackRock,* (2021) https://www.blackrock.com/corporate/investor-relations/larry-fink-ceo-letter

177   Elizabeth Diltz Marshall, "Goldman Sachs Pledges $750 Million to Environmental Causes by 2030," November 16, 2019 https://www.reuters.com/article/goldman-sachs-environment/goldman-sachs-pledges-750-billion-to-environmental-causes-by-2030-idUSL1N28Q0RL

178   Goldman Sachs "Climate Change," (Unknown) https://www.goldmansachs.com/citizenship/environmental-stewardship/documents/climate-change-highlights.pdf

179   Brad Smith, "Microsoft Will be Carbon Negative by 2030,"

Microsoft Blog, (January 16, 2020) https://blogs.microsoft.com/blog/2020/01/16/microsoft-will-be-carbon-negative-by-2030/

180   Brad Smith, "Microsoft launches initiative to help 25 million people worldwide acquire the digital skills needed in a COVID-19 economy," *Microsoft Blog*, (June 30, 2020) "https://blogs.microsoft.com/blog/2020/06/30/microsoft-launches-initiative-to-help-25-million-people-worldwide-acquire-the-digital-skills-needed-in-a-covid-19-economy/

181   Google, "Our Commitments," (2020) https://sustainability.google/commitments/

182   Philanthropy News Digest, "Google Commits $175 million to Racial Equity Initiatives," (June 19, 2020) https://philanthropynewsdigest.org/news/google-commits-175-million-to-racial-equity-initiatives

183   Apple, "Apple Commits to be 100 Percent Carbon Neutral for its Products and Supply Chain by 2030," *Apple Newsroom* (July 21, 2020) https://www.apple.com/newsroom/2020/07/apple-commits-to-be-100-percent-carbon-neutral-for-its-supply-chain-and-products-by-2030/

184   Apple, "Apple Launches Major New Racial Equity and Justice Initiative Projects to Challnege Systemic Racism, Advance Racial Equity Nationwide," *Apple Newsroom* (January 31, 2021) https://www.apple.com/newsroom/2021/01/apple-launches-major-new-racial-equity-and-justice-initiative-projects-to-challenge-systemic-racism-advance-racial-equity-nationwide/

185   Facebook Sustainability, "We Are Committed to Reaching Net Zero Emissions Across Our Value Chain in 2030," (2021) https://sustainability.fb.com/

186   Jay Peters, "Facebook Commits $200 Million to Support Black-Owned Businesses," *The Verge*, (June 18, 2020) https://www.theverge.com/2020/6/18/21296110/facebook-200-million-lift-black-voices-businesses-creators-diversity

187   Tesla, "Carbon Impact," (2021) https://www.tesla.com/carbonimpact

188   Madeline Cuff, "Tesla Benchmarks its Carbon Emissions for the

First Time," *GreenBiz,* (April 25, 2019) https://www.greenbiz.com/article/
tesla-benchmarks-its-carbon-impact-first-time

189   Tesla, "Diversity, Equity, and Impact Report 2020 (US)," (2021)
https://www.tesla.com/sites/default/files/downloads/2020-DEI-impact-re-
port.pdf

190   Amazon Sustainability, "All In: Staying On Course to Our
Commitment to Sustainability," (2021) https://sustainability.aboutam-
azon.com/?energyType=true&workerCount=true&engagementPro-
gram=true&productCategory=true

191   Annie Palmer, "Amazon Wins Naming Rights to New Seattle Stadi-
um," *CNBC,* (June 25, 2020) https://www.cnbc.com/2020/06/25/amazon-
wins-naming-rights-to-new-seattle-stadium-climate-pledge-arena.html

192   Taylor Nicole Rogers, "The Giving Pledge could be worth $600
billion by 2022," *Business Insider* (October 2019)
https://www.businessinsider.com/billionaire-signed-giving-pledge-isnt-
growing-rapidly-as-hoped-2019-10#:~:text=The%20Giving%20Pledge%20
could%20be,according%20to%20the%20organization's%20website.

193   Dominic Rushe, "Jeff Bezos Tells Employees 'One Day Amazon
Will Fail,'" *The Guardian,* November 16, 2018, https://www.theguardian.
com/technology/2018/nov/16/jeff-bezos-amazon-will-fail-recording-report

194   Brian Whitworth, "Socio-Tehnical Design System," *Interaction
Design Foundation,* (2021) https://www.interaction-design.org/literature/
book/the-encyclopedia-of-human-computer-interaction-2nd-ed/socio-tech-
nical-system-design

195   "Sustainable Development Goals," United Nations Development
Programme, July 1, 2020 https://www.undp.org/content/undp/en/home/sus-
tainable-development-goals.html#:~:text=The%20Sustainable%20Develop-
ment%20Goals%20(SDGs,peace%20and%20prosperity%20by%202030.

A free ebook edition is available with the purchase of this book.

To claim your free ebook edition:

1. Visit MorganJamesBOGO.com
2. Sign your name CLEARLY in the space
3. Complete the form and submit a photo of the entire copyright page
4. You or your friend can download the ebook to your preferred device

A **FREE** ebook edition is available for you or a friend with the purchase of this print book.

CLEARLY SIGN YOUR NAME ABOVE

Instructions to claim your free ebook edition:
1. Visit MorganJamesBOGO.com
2. Sign your name CLEARLY in the space above
3. Complete the form and submit a photo of this entire page
4. You or your friend can download the ebook to your preferred device

Print & Digital Together Forever.

Snap a photo

Free ebook

Read anywhere